PRAISE FOR *MUSIC*

Music in the Halls is not a book that you can prepare yourself to read; maybe I was a little overly ambitious, thinking I could absorb it all in one sitting. From the introduction, the reader is drawn into the author's world, one of high pressure/high stakes, where immediate outcomes are demanded. *Music in the Halls* is a memoir, documentary, and wakeup call neatly packaged into one text. In turning the pages, Lean on Me, Spike Lee, and Abbott Elementary are pictured in my mind. Jankowski's book is one of intimacy, crying, violence, anger, animalistic desperation and isolation. Jankowski confronts us repeatedly, which education do we want? Which education do we value? "We expect a curiosity for learning to magically spring from this turbulent terrain filled with imminent, real, and embedded danger. We are the fools." And now, after the COVID-19 pandemic, virtual learning, and every assortment of challenge known to human beings, this book, this call to action is more relevant than before. Do not simply put down this book after you have read the last word. Decide in this moment how you will live with a focus on "social emotional needs more than strict education."

– Marja Humphrey, PhD, NCC, LGPC Assistant Professor, School Counseling Bowie State University

Being a teacher in a public school at times is like being a juror in a courtroom. One can be caught listening and watching not realizing that more than a witness (or parent) that one is responsible for justice—in this case the education of our youth. In his book *Music in the Halls*, Bernard Jankowski, a special education teacher in a DC public school, soon learns that all children must be considered special if the job of teaching is taking seriously. It's unfortunate that so much is broken in our educational system. Jankowski provides written testimony as to how educational experiments too often fail. *Music in the Halls* is filled with a symphony of children stories. Jankowski has an ear and a heart for his students. It's impossible to read this book without swaying or shuckling with sadness. This book will make one pray for change in our school systems.

— E. Ethelbert Miller, writer and literary activist

I have known Bernard Jankowski's writing in all its forms over the years, and in no way was I prepared to read a book of such consummate humanity and prowess as *Music in the Halls*. I began to scan the text to get a generalized understanding; and then found myself riveted to every word on every paragraph through every page; the story is like a knife you hold in your hand that you can't let go, and must be held carefully.

The book is one large conceit for the wound in our society but told through the brown eyes of the children and the broken hearts of their teachers. Society's wretched wound is the classroom where teachers are heroes or failures, or both, against inestimable odds of poverty, hunger, anger and shame. The organization of the book is a masterful structure for the "teaching poverty" experience with anecdotes, quotes, stories, characters, situations, tolerances, authority, traditions, customs. And, more than anything, a try for what can be saved.

In my younger years I taught in the lower grades. My classes were made of children who came to school well- dressed after a hearty breakfast, and yet the stressors were always enormous. I cannot imagine navigating the lifelines that were extended in "Mr. J's" book. I see those many faces with all those children's names, as straining and struggling toward some sort of hope as if it is the sun- yet so out of reach.

"Will you be my dad tomorrow, Mr. J?" Bernard Jankowski was that and more, but took away words burned on his soul: "Happy Now, Sad Later." How do we get every member of Congress to read this book? Nevertheless, I am confident that

Music in the Halls will reach many readers who are passionate about children and education, not only for the profound statements, but for its emotional purity and rasp. It is a Masterwork. A Masterwork.

– Grace Cavalieri, Maryland poet Laureate

In *Music in the Halls*, Bernard Jankowski, "Mr. J" to his students, taught at Amidon Elementary School, in southwest Washington DC. This book digs into and displays the raw emotion and reality of that world laid against the everydayness of school. You feel the children's pain and the teachers' frustrations. You feel the inability of the container to hold the energy of widespread poverty, trauma, and PTSD. Mr. J reached deep into himself to give to his students all he had of empathy, intelligence, sympathy, and love. He fed them when they could not speak from hunger and waited beside them when they were mute from last night's terrors. He brought to the chaos of their lives, and their parents' lives, respect and learning and a resolute spirit of uncommon compassion.

– Mary Ann Larkin, Emeritus, Howard University

Music in the Halls provides a searing and indelible portrait of life as an educator in the DC public schools. Bernard Jankowski embeds the reader in the unrelenting chaos of DC Public Schools through a series of dispatches from the frontlines. This basketball poet's finely tuned ear presents a hallway music that is heartbreakingly sad, at times joyous and full of humor. Jankowski covers an American tragedy that is systemic in its continual neglect of the children who most need someone to stand up for them.

– Dean Smith, author of *Baltimore Sons*

Using vivid portraits, *Music in the Halls* reveals in telling detail the trauma of high poverty children. Jankowski captures the cultural dissonance and stressors, the generational trauma and

PTSD, and the challenges of teaching with striking scenes, character portraits and essays. For people working in this environment, this book will motivate you to bring your best self into the school building each and every day. These children deserve nothing less.

– Dr. Dwayne E. Ham, Sr. Adjunct Professor, Bowie State University

MUSIC IN THE HALLS

The Heart and Heartbreak of Teaching at a
High-Poverty School in Washington, DC

Bernard Jankowski

Pact Press

Published by Pact Press
An imprint of
Regal House Publishing, LLC
Raleigh, NC 27605
All rights reserved

https://fitzroybooks.com
Printed in the United States of America

ISBN -13 (paperback): 9781646034246
ISBN -13 (epub): 9781646034253
Library of Congress Control Number: 2023934868

Cover design by © C. B. Royal

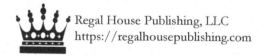

Regal House Publishing, LLC
https://regalhousepublishing.com

Printed in the United States of America

In memory of Cheryl W. Haynes,
a champion for all children

AUTHOR'S NOTE

This book is based upon my five years of experience as a teacher and Special Education Coordinator at Amidon-Bowen Elementary School in Southwest, Washington, DC. While not a strict chronology of those years, the book loosely follows the timeline from summer training and my first year to my final year in DCPS. The book is structured predominately around topics central to poverty and education: children, teachers, education reform, bureaucracy, trauma, violence, and the community. I recreated events, locales, and conversations from notes and memories. In order to maintain their anonymity, I have changed the names of individuals. Amidon-Bowen Elementary is referred to in the book as Amidon Elementary, or simply Amidon.

Special thanks to my wife and editor, Kathy, who held me strong throughout and is always an inspiration. Also, to Mary Ann Larkin and Patric Pepper for their encouragement and keen editorial advice. Finally, to all those at Amidon-Bowen Elementary School who worked shoulder-to-shoulder to put children first.

DR. DAWYNE E. HAM

Adjunct Professor, Bowie State University

Contributing the Foreword

Dr. Ham is currently an elementary school counselor in Montgomery county public schools. He is also an adjunct professor in the department of counseling at Bowie State University, teaching in the school psychology program. He has also taught courses at the University of Maryland College Park in group counseling and supervision. In addition to being a school counselor Dr. Ham has been an assistant principal in Montgomery County and the District of Columbia public schools where he met Bernard Jankowski. He has also served as interim principal during a time when his principal was on extended leave.

Dr. Ham has also presented at state, regional and national conferences and published on issues concerning African American boys and college going cultures. He has a masters degree in counselor education from North Carolina A&T, an advanced certificate in supervision and counseling from the University of Maryland and a doctorate in educational leadership from Bowie State University.

He enjoys his family and friends, especially his two boys, one of which is an Eagle Scout and his other son who is a First Class Boy Scout. He has a lovely wife, also Dr. Ham who teaches in the department of counseling as a full-time faculty professor.

Dr. Marja Humphrey

Assistant Professor in the School Counseling program
at Bowie State University

Contributing the Epilogue

Dr. Humphrey, an assistant professor in the school counseling program at Bowie State University, prepares graduate students to work professionally with students, families and individuals in urban communities. Her research interests include counselor preparation, leadership, wellness, and online learning. She has taught, advised, and counseled K-12 students, college students with disabilities, and adults with depression, anxiety, and substance use disorders. A coauthor of *Elements of Culture in Counseling*, a multicultural counseling text, and several published articles, Dr. Humphrey has also presented at state, regional and national conferences.

In addition to her research and teaching, Dr. Humphrey serves on various committees at the department, college, and university levels. She advises several student organizations (the BSU chapter of the Maryland School Counselor Association, the African Psychology Student Association, and Make a Wish). Dr. Humphrey co-chairs the interfaith faculty team at Bowie State University. This team was awarded two grants to further their cooperative work on campus with students, faculty, and staff, building bridges across differences and increasing interfaith literacy. She also currently serves as the treasurer-elect with the Maryland Counseling Association and represents Bowie State University as a board member with the Maryland Consortium for adjunct faculty professional development.

Personally committed to dialogue as an effective way to engage others in cross-cultural understanding, Dr. Humphrey consults with and has provided training for mental health agencies, private businesses, and community organizations. When not working, she is an avid reader, and enjoys time connecting with her family and friends over great food and music.

FOREWORD

Bernard Jankowski's book, *Music in the Halls*, is set within the direct aftermath of the chaotic transition of the DC Public School system to Michelle Rhee's IMPACT Evaluation system. I served as the assistant principal at Amidon-Bowen Elementary, a high-poverty, low-performing school for the five years that Mr. Jankowski taught there as a special education teacher and served as part-time special education coordinator (from 2011-2016). This book displays the confusion and disruption of that time and how adults, children, and families are ill-served when the system tilts excessively toward unrealistic data metrics over the very real and significant challenges of children growing up in poverty.

The underperformance of the District of Columbia Public School (DCPS) system was exacerbated in 2007 when the council provided the mayor, Adrian Fenty, an ill-equipped individual who didn't understand school systems, the power to make broad educational decisions. His appointment of Michelle Rhee as chancellor of DCPS led to systemic failures, particularly in the neediest schools, that adversely affected the lives of hundreds of teachers and thousands of school children.

At the start of Rhee's reign, hundreds of long-term, experienced teachers, mainly Black, were fired. The District of Columbia's task of providing a quality education was now being evaluated by Rhee's IMPACT system, focused on teachers' evaluations and schools' standardized test scores, making every adult in a school responsible for radically improving student achievement data. This racially biased system set unrealistic bars for the mainly Black teachers that were teaching in the most difficult and underfunded schools.

Despite IMPACT, the children in Wards 7 and 8, the most impoverished children, were still failing. Every year from 2007 to

2011, more than 200 teachers would be fired during the summer, leaving the school district floundering to find qualified bodies to educate the nations capital's poor and illiterate students. This was happening at the precipice of a national teacher shortage. Randi Weingarten, the president of the American Federation of Teachers, criticized the IMPACT evaluation system at the time and what she called the chancellor's "destructive cycle of hire, fire, repeat." "Evaluations should include a component of student learning, of course, but there also has to be teacher development and support," Ms. Weingarten said. "It can't just be a 'gotcha' system, like the one in DC."[1]

Data from the District of Columbia Office of the state superintendent reports that in the city's poorest communities, the schools in Wards 7 and 8, only 8 percent of the students reached a level 4 or 5 on the PARCC assessment (met or exceeded expectations) in mathematics from 2011-2016.[2] These same students were even less successful in reading. Did the impact of a mayor-appointed chancellor help to support the impoverished children who continue to fail generationally? The definitive answer is no.

The Washington Post reported in 2018 that "Eight years after Rhee's arrival, poor and minority students were still far less likely to have an effective teacher in their classroom and perform at grade level. Achievement gaps were as wide as ever: about 60 percent of poor Black students were below proficient in math and reading and had made only marginal gains since the changes were made."[3]

Schools in wealthier neighborhoods like Maury, Thomas, Eaton, Alice Deal, and Hearst often outpace Title 1 schools in funding. These schools historically have Parent-Teacher Associations that give money and are competent enough to

1 Tamar Lewin, "School Chief Dismisses 241 Teachers in Washington." *New York Times*, July 23, 2010.
2 Although in Ward 6, Amidon-Bowen Elementary mirrors many of the schools in Wards 7 and 8 (academically and demographically).
3 Emma Brown, Valerie Strauss, and Perry Stein, "It was hailed as the national model for school reform. Then the scandals hit." *Washington Post*, March 10, 2018.

solicit and plead for more funding. Inequities in the district are perpetuated and support the already wealthy parts of the city. Who gives voice to the voiceless? Are we in the *education business* or the *business of education*? There is a difference!

Unfortunately, DCPS is mainly in the business of education. Their evaluation system didn't support a holistic approach or accept a pace of realistic gradual change. If you drink the IMPACT Kool-Aid, and believe it to be red with sugar, then you will believe that the DC Public School system is working effectively to improve student achievement.

There were times when it was obvious that the school system was trying to integrate, begging high-income parents into those wards that historically enrolled fewer white students and more Black and brown ones. Yet, affluent parents rarely lived in Ward 7 and 8 and, if by chance they did, we did not see their children in those public schools. They would opt instead to take the long road trip to schools in Northwest and Northeast DC.

This flight from neighborhood schools was thwarted in 2016 when the school district started making it necessary to protect their blue ribbon, well-funded schools with rules that made it difficult for some students to enroll. Charter schools were the preliminary answer for families facing this dilemma. Then charter schools began kicking difficult or underperforming students out just after the October 1 enrollment deadline (once they received their funding based on those enrollment numbers). These schools did not want to have to deal with the students who had behavioral challenges or required special education. Time and time again, the poorest children, the ones who need the most help, were kicked to the curb.

The academic involvement and social-emotional support of our children, Black and brown, with generationally low academic success requires a special person, one that despite their training was going to stick it out and do whatever it took to ensure their success. That person is Bernard Jankowski. A graduate of the DC Teaching Fellows program, he was expected to make a difference in one of the toughest impoverished schools in the District of Columbia Public Schools. He arrived at Amidon-Bowen in 2011 with the desire to improve the academic success of those students. Although many teachers quit, some on the first day, Mr. Jankowski stayed for five years to ensure the success of students in special education that might have never realized their potential without Mr. J.!

Mr. Jankowski gives insight into the fight he decided to take on as a white man who truly cares about the plight of brown and black kids, often boys, who were placed in special education. These children—third, fourth, and fifth graders, many reading on a kindergarten level—were the students who fought, cursed, and missed school because for them, school was not the first thing nor the appropriate social system that supported their success. School reminded them what they couldn't do, how they were not enough. This white man was committed to changing the mindset and trajectory for these Black students with his love, compassion, and heart, qualities that are often missing even for teachers whose race mirrors these impoverished students. Not Mr. J.

Dwayne E. Ham, Sr., Ed D
Adjunct Professor, Bowie State University

INTRODUCTION

GROUND ZERO

As I enter this world, I know that this is ground zero of the educational experiment. Under the microscope, the lowest of the low, you know them as high-poverty, low-performing schools. Smack dab in the middle of the nationwide debate on education, these are tales from within those walls. Our job? To improve the kids' reading and math levels—not tomorrow, not over a reasonable amount of time, but NOW.

Connecting the building and all of us—students, teachers, administrators, janitors, clerical staff—is a high-tension wire. Everyone is on high alert; all are under constant observation (sometimes by multiple parties). Events here end up in the news (good, bad, or ugly). We are measured, prodded, poked, analyzed, observed everyone knows and has internalized the importance of the task: to educate these kids. No one is exactly sure what to do or what should be done to make the urgency productive and viable. Ideas are thrown at us left and right. Central Office tosses new concepts at the walls and then watches us dance to see what sticks. We are the test tube, the crucible. Everything is in flux, everything is in disarray, nothing is consistent, nothing is coherent. In this environment, you teach a group of students, many academically below grade level, who, if properly evaluated, would qualify for special education interventions. Resource poor, mission driven, fragmented, incoherent, idealistic, unrealistic, hyper-focused, unfocused: DCPS.

1

ACROSS THE GREAT DIVIDE

Sharpening Pencils

Ms. Wilson looks at me, a white man "across the river" in DC, shakes her head and laughs. "Ha! Keep hope alive! Keep hope alive!" Then, "Can you take care of these?" handing me a dozen pencils. She nods to the sharpener. So, this is how it begins, student teaching. I'm an apprentice again, a middle-aged man in training. I've scrubbed pots for cooks, lugged wood for carpenters, humped brick for bricklayers, proofed copy for editors, learned business negotiations from dot-com wolves, and it's come full circle to pencils again, pencils, still the instrument of communication.

My preparation for the adventure ahead was elementary summer school. Could I remember elementary school? Using pencils? I walked over to the sharpener and looked out the window from Randle Highlands Elementary. As the morning haze of dawn lifted from the hills, I saw the majesty of DC across the Anacostia River, the monuments, and the Capitol standing proud. But were these institutions blind? Why this divide? What was this world? Here, across the river.

Already, I was impressed with the beauty of Anacostia, the rolling hills, and the tree-lined streets. Through the lens of the news and stories from friends, I had imagined it some Bronx-like landscape of gutted-out buildings and empty warehouses. Quite the contrary, the area looked green and friendly. Why this disjunct? What was going on? What had happened here? Here I was, among the stories of Anacostia, the roughest place in DC, notorious for drive-bys, murders, robberies, and drugs. Here, in the middle of it, soon there would be thirty kids surrounding me, all Black, and me, white. Divides, divides, what divides us? Myths of pencils. Myths of DC. Myths of Anacostia. Of white and Black, rich and poor, powerful and powerless. From the other side of the river, my new education was about to begin. I was being sharpened, clarified.

Who Is This White Man?

Drowsy Summer School morning, the southern sun of DC sifts through the windows. Here with a real class now, time to teach.

The thirty first graders are a mix of sleepiness, squirmy energy, and bright-eyed hope. As we go over our morning routines and rules, the procession starts.

All day, the other summer school teachers stop by to catch a peek, check out my room. To see what this white man is doing with their Black babies. Observing this curious spectacle like a freak show, a car wreck, or a rare bird.

The Real Work Begins

Here at Amidon Elementary in Southwest DC, as the official academic year begins, the school is all shook up. They cleaned out the old staff and administration. A few remnants remain: a battle-tested teacher here and there, one holdover from administrative support, and two custodians. They escaped the "Grim Reaper," as these survivors called her. She was known in the news as Michelle Rhee, who descended on the DC school system with her scythe named IMPACT.

More than a dozen new teachers and a first-time principal confront students from more than another culture; this is a whole other world. I was dual certified in elementary general education and special education. I had received my rigorous training in the DC Teaching Fellows program. I wasn't trained for this, could not have been trained for the open defiance, the cursing right up in my face. On the first morning, a child stops in the hall, looks up at me, yells, "I'm going to kill you."

One teacher, who came all the way from California, resigns by lunchtime, said, "I don't trust myself with these kids."

The children hang in the doorways of the classrooms, sometimes three or more of them clutching to each other and the door. Little packs of kids stampede down the halls, giggling and flailing their arms. Beneath the water fountain, a child weeps as other kids get a drink and the water dripping from the pipes melds with the tears streaming down her face. Turn the corner, and three kids are brawling, hitting, cursing at each other in a blur of action. Another pack of crying children sits against the wall in the hallway.

Into the library where kids dance on top of the bookshelves throwing books at each other, running around the shelves squealing as the librarian yips after them in hot pursuit. Others are tipping the reading chairs over. One child has hoisted a chair above his head and runs to smash the window. Throughout all of this, adults are barking and shouting, grabbing kids' arms, scolding kids, getting in their faces, yelling for them to STOP! Look in one room and kids are running around on top of the tables. They have torn paper into bits, using the air blowing up from the air conditioner to blow confetti all over the room. Kids stab each other with pencils, waving their book bags around and hitting each other. Some are beneath desks, shaking and crying. You see it all and can't see it all. Mayhem rules, kids are frayed, some faces gleeful with mischief, others in shock or grief. As I wandered dazed down the hall, Ms. Bluette reached out of her classroom and pulled me inside, "C'mere, buddy. You're working with me."

The Good Ship Bluette

Ms. Bluette's room was immaculate. An experienced teacher, her walls were festooned with positive messages and the bookshelves full of leveled reading books laid out and ready to be explored. She'd made sure there was a considerable supply of African-American literature, so the kids could learn about *their own* history, *their own* courage, *their own* stories. When the first bell rang and the kids shuffled in, she asked her new class, "You see those windows? Why do you think there are grates on those windows?" Puzzled, the kids looked back at the window. "Because I throw kids out there. You want to play with me? That's what will happen. *Boop!* (she flicked her thumb and forefinger) Out the window!" So, the lines of order were drawn. The kids knew better than to take Ms. Bluette to her breaking point, to take Ms. Bluette "there."

My first day in her classroom flew by in a blur of faces and names. The speed of the classroom environment was a jolt to me. I was constantly surrounded by kids, thirty of them jammed in this room with two adults. The air conditioning in the room was broken and the thick late August air drifted through the open windows. Beads of sweat formed on mine and the kids' brows. Every hour, we took a much-needed water break. Like a ship at sea for the day, traveling through time, traveling through words, letters, sounds and Ms. Bluette's tales of how education changed her life and could change yours, too, if (and she said "IF") you stop playing around. Then in the afternoon, we did math and clapped out multiplication tables. I was wiped out by three o'clock and was relieved when the bell rang, and the kids lined up to go home. But at times, I saw real education taking place and saw a glow over the class and over Ms. Bluette. I felt a warmth and a hope and a feeling that I had come home. How was this possible? Me? Home? Here?

New Year—Old Beefs

I walked downstairs with Ms. Bluette as the kids were being released, took a deep breath, and tapped her on the shoulder. "I feel lucky, lucky to be here, lucky that I was teamed with you," I told her.

Ms. Bluette glanced back with a smile. "Talk to me in a few weeks."

Down in the lobby, kids were running in every direction, little ones right out to the city streets. Some of them with their siblings holding on tight, others crying for their mothers. When, out of nowhere, I heard shattering glass and turned to see two girls fighting. Jaylen had Zaria shoved up against the school trophy case and trophies crashed to the ground and shards of glass were everywhere. Jaylen grabbed Zaria's face in her fingers and twisted her mouth and nose. There was blood on the tiles and crying and tears and screams of "Take it back! I'll kill you bitch." "No! Your dead folks!" "Your dead folks!" back and forth "Your dead folks!" until the security guard stepped in and broke it up.

Zaria was gasping for breath, weeping tears of confusion, anger, and fear. I took her aside and asked what had happened.

"She talked about my dead folks."

"What?" I replied, confused.

Ms. Raynes, the school counselor with years of experience in DC schools, said, "I got this Mr. J." She stepped in and comforted Zaria with her gentle tone until she was well enough to go home.

Later, she explained the situation to me. "You don't talk about two things down here—people's mothers and their dead folks. That's what this is about. Those two families have a long-standing beef. Zaria's father shot and killed Jaylen's father for stealing his woman from him and now he's in jail. That was seven years ago, but still the families are at each other, can't put it to rest. But thanks for trying, Mr. J. I did see your light today you know."

"My what?" I asked.

"Your light. I do that. I see auras. A few times today, when you were helping the kids and when you reached out to Zaria, I saw your aura. You're a good one, Mr. J. You'll be all right."

This only added to the ending confusion of the day. My light? Long-held beefs? A few minutes earlier, I had felt at home but now the mystery of this place, the foreignness of it settled over me. Would I be able to find my way? I stood out on the school stoop and watched the last little ones trickle off and disappear.

I Drive from One World to Another

I leave my quiet, comfortable suburban home around six each morning. My path to work takes me past the McMansions and real mansions of Potomac, houses big enough to hold a dozen of the Southwest DC families or more. The whole inequity of wealth is displayed in gaudy fashion before me, mansions with garages bigger than townhomes. Through the town of Potomac, I swoop down the George Washington Parkway past Turkey Run, past the mythical Three Sisters rocks in the Potomac River, and see the grand old city. The eloquent design that lays before me masks the chaos and confusion that rules the neighborhoods where my kids live. Georgetown University is perched proudly on the hills like privilege and erudition itself. Each brick laid a monument to wealth and the education it affords. The old buildings of stone and the new ones of glass fill the available river view property. Then across Memorial Bridge, past the statue of Lincoln and then Jefferson, with the Washington Monument and the White House beyond. It's all built on noble words like freedom and resolve. Even the street names portray this pride: Independence, Constitution. Then past the colorful and lively fish markets of Maine Avenue and deep into the heart of Southwest.

There's also a different history within these city borders, the ghetto history of slavery, Jim Crow, poverty, and distress. It's a hodgepodge, the waterfront neighborhood, amid gentrification, with the Arena Stage nearby, a new Safeway and office buildings, the waterfront a few blocks away, and these kids stranded or forgotten, locked into this island within Southwest, bearing the brunt of intergenerational poverty on their little shoulders. Southwest is a playground to them. I was astonished on my first day how, at the close of the school day, the children were set free into the city. Responsible youngsters walk their little brothers and sisters safely home. At the end of the day, if you got between the children and their siblings, they'll fall into an all-out panic. Their resolve to accomplish this mission is absolute. They will find their little brother or sister; asking anyone and everyone until the little bopper finally pops out. Then they'll smile and say, "C'mon, you okay?" and hold their hands tightly all the way home.

The disparity of wealth will make you retch. To drive past houses where a team of landscapers is working on someone's lawn to neighborhoods where the kids can't afford decent food and clothes is appalling. We sit here in school, eight blocks from the United States Capitol building, day after day facing these monstrous gaps. This problem—born of slavery and Jim Crow, of culture gaps and language gaps, of huge money gaps, and in the end, of skin color—persists. It is woven into the spoken words and the body language of the children. They feel the failure and know, consciously or not, that they don't stack up. The stress of not measuring up invades their lives from morning to night: obsession with flashy shoes, celebrities, cheap images on TV, well-off people on the street. We know what we know, we do what we do, and a few blocks down the street the machinery of government flails away and works relentlessly to cast a blind eye, maintain the status quo, and further line the pockets of the top one percent.

Learning the Language of Poverty

To survive here, I need to understand these children. Feel where they are coming from. I am a stranger in a strange land. I'm learning a new language: the language of poverty. I need to see through the kids' eyes, understand their world if I'm ever going to be an effective teacher for them. I'm learning fragments of their reality; I have yet to piece it together into a whole.

Poverty Is a Gnawing Pit

It starts in the stomach. A need unfed. It becomes a headache, a heartache, a need to sleep, to shut it all off. Exhaustion sets in. Confusion. Disillusion. The basics of the day are not there. There is a fear with that hunger, a fear that needs will not be met. A fear of survival. A death fear. An animal fear. I see it in their eyes. A hollowness. A hopelessness. Little children walking around with old, weary souls. How do we expect these kids to learn?

Poverty is Alert

The eyes of poverty catch everything, see every shiny object, case a room in a second and know if there's something new or valuable around. Teachers know not to leave phones and iPads around. These kids know where you hide your snacks and candy. Poverty is shifty and quick. A hungry stomach will lie. A deprived child will trust no one. Survival follows no rules.

Poverty Treasures What It Can Get

When you have nothing, the smallest thing can be a huge prize. These children treasure the tiniest things. I could keep a whole room in check with the promise of a few Cheerios. The kids will hoard what you give them, will fight until blood flows. They know their things, the objects that are theirs. And food? Or a treat? This is like a jewel. They will find the very best child inside of them and be that kid for that reward. And when they get it? They will relish that prize. They will make the moment last. They eat with tiny bites, treasure and savor the taste and the relaxation that comes from not being in want. For a while they are not in survival mode. For the moment, their immediate needs are met.

Poverty Is Physical

High-poverty kids are very physical. They move together pushing, shoving, slapping each other. Their pure physicality is a way of establishing bonds and hierarchy. It is vital for a teacher to establish physical boundaries. Children are everywhere. You will turn and a child will hug you or playfully push you. You need to be firm, maintain your personal space, let students know appropriate boundaries.

2

THE CHILDREN, THE CHILDREN

Vivid Names, Etched Faces

I came home from work in a daze, lay in bed, and stared at the wall. This first week, I felt more like a bouncer than a teacher. I forgot how many fights I had broken up. My wife called up, "You okay up there?"

"Yea, I guess," I replied.

In the swirling silence, the bedroom walls became screens, and the screens became lit up with the faces, their intensity, vibrancy, and pain. I had been dropped into a wild shook-up world, and I was shaken up. As I followed the phantasms on the walls, I put names to the kids' faces. I had never been good at remembering names before, but in this first week, I had learned fifty or more. I whispered the familiar: John, Matthew, Robert, William, Rose; and then the foreign: JaiBre, Jai'la, Jamika, Tiara, Yaqub, Iesha. Each name conjuring up the etched truth of a face full of joy, hope, and sorrow

Street Urchins

I've seen them in movies and heard news stories about them but had never lived daily with true street urchins. The ones that come into the elementary school bedraggled, sleepy, starving. Thank goodness for the free meals here; the urchins are the kids that come every day. They need to eat, and their parents, or whomever they slept with, kick them out and send them on their way no matter how sick or filthy they are. You can smell the weed in their clothes and see it in their little bloodshot eyes, starting the day already without hope, stoned, or wasted, or starving, or exhausted, or all the above.

"What's up with your shoes, cuz?" or "You're dirty" are the sharpest insults thrown at the urchins. The shame is shown in the kids' sagging shoulders, their untied shoes, their furtive eyes searching the room with a laser-beam focus for any food item, even a food wrapper, to stick into their starving mouths to chew on something to ease the pain.

The night is their time of freedom, their time to howl, to feel alive, their time of goofing and living dangerously with their crew. Shoplifting, jumping people, stealing bikes, hopping the subways, woofing at adults, together now running the streets and then catch a little sleep before breakfast at school. Often, a few are sitting on the steps of the school at early dawn before anyone else has arrived, even in the freezing cold. Their hungry eyes wait for an adult to open the door to the only warmth, safety, and security they know in this world.

The Boy with a Thousand Faces

What war are we fighting here?
Are we at war with ourselves?
Trying to ram knowledge down kids' throats?
What knowledge? What thoughts? Whose mind? Which
     history? What civilization?
Is this the white man's tongue being spit back out?
Columbus Day! Thanksgiving!

The boy with a thousand faces doesn't know and doesn't care.
He smiles like a gremlin,
his head like a bumpy rock
from all the hard knocks.
Shirt hasn't been washed in a week.
Then there's the stomach aches,
hides a toothache, too.
They say Mom's going to rehab.
Still, each night,
he's running those streets.

Instruction starts,
the boy with a thousand faces
just leans back and smiles
a brand-new smile.

Janeya and Akeelah and the Bee

Janeya hated to read, hated to write. She was a "hall runner." Her first goal in class was to get out of class. She could always find someone to pick with, someone to help her stir it up. She'd cry or they'd cry, and she'd be taken from class to the social worker's office or would walk the halls. That drama was less stressful for her than having to face her lack of reading skills, so she used her inner intelligence, her survival tactic of self-preservation. But the days stack up, and Janeya got further and further behind. Too many days out of class and before you know it, you fall a few years behind.

But today was different. Today we had free tickets to Arena Stage and here we were seated in the plush seats with the buzz of a play, *Akeelah and the Bee*, about to appear before our eyes. Janeya took her seat, her eyes glued on the stage. The kids swayed and sang to the songs before the play started. They knew every word. Then, Akeelah appeared. There was no space between Janeya and the stage. She was riveted. Her face beamed. Akeelah was studying and learning with all her might, doing it for Janeya, who struggled mightily with her spelling. With every spelling bee victory, Akeelah was washing away Janeya's deficiencies. She was a hero, brave and capable. Janeya followed Akeelah step by step down her path of self-actualization. For a while, she even felt that she was that bright girl showing the world what a little Black girl can do when she sets her mind to it. When the play was over, Janeya turned to me beaming. "Can we stay and see that again?"

The Anger

The little boy is mad. Really mad. Again.
   "Kalil, why are you always upset? What's bothering you?"
Kalil spits back, "I'm angry. Whatcha think?"
"Angry at what?"
He turned and looked me in the eye,
"Damn, Mr. J.!" his voice squeaked. "Angry at everything!"

The Crying Behind the Door

I walk to class and hear weeping, a child crying. I look behind the door and there's Jazmin, tears streaming down her cheeks. Her two big eyes stare up at me and I offer her a hand. It's my planning period, so I bring her in my room and ask, "Feel like talking?"
   "No," she replied.
   "Why don't you pick a book off the shelf? Just sit awhile and read." She grabs a book and tucks into the cozy reading chair. "Whatcha reading?" I ask.
   "Poetry, jus' poetry."
   "You like that?"
She sobs a bit more, then meets my eyes. "Yes, I do."
   "Good. You have time, no rush."
She asks for a pencil and paper and begins to copy Blake's poem down line for line:

> Then they followed,
> Where the vision led:
> And saw their sleeping child,
> Among tygers wild.
> To this day they dwell
> In a lonely dell
> Nor fear the wolvish howl,
> Nor the lions growl.

"Why do they spell it t-y-g-e-r-s? It should be t-i-g-e-r-s, right?"

"That's from back in the day, old English."

"Oh."

"You feeling better?"

"Yea, fine," she responds.

With each line she writes, the sobbing softens.

Lavon by the Water Fountain

He hasn't spoken to any adult in months. A *selective mute* is how they classify his condition. He's a big kid and I work for months at building a relationship with him. I bring him to my room, give him a cookie. He speaks! "Thanks," he says in a surprisingly high and squeaky voice. That's all for conversation today. I want to ask him why he won't speak to anyone, but I don't want to stretch my luck.

He won't go to class, refuses to do any work. He stands at the water fountain for hours. Kids come up and he nods, turns it on for them, gives them their water. He refuses some, the bullies, or those who have done him wrong. This is all he can offer for now, this water.

The Boy Who Drives Books

When it's time to read, he chooses a book, not to read but to drive. He walks over to the reading area, plops down in his drivers' seat and he's off on a new adventure. He's talking on the phone getting traffic conditions and directions to his next pickup, shifts the gears, the book is his steering wheel. He turns it round and round. He wants to be a truck driver or a policeman, shifts gears again, gets his next job on the phone, responds, "I gotcha covered."

Out on the playground, he arrests a kid. Pulls out his make-believe gun and jams it in the little boy's back, then walks him up against the fence and ties his hands with his shoelaces. He warns the boy: "Don't move or I'll shoot. I will use this gun!"

Kayshawn Asks

Father's Saturday is this weekend. Kayshawn comes to school filthy, clothes torn, unwashed, skin gray, "all ashy," as they say. The depths of his eyes hold pain in deep wells. When he gets triggered, Kayshawn hits and screams and sobs. Even when he's fighting, he's crying. And Mom, a crackhead, is barely there for him. Maybe not crack now, sometimes dippers, a joint dipped in PCP. I have bizarre parent-teacher conferences with her, trying to talk about the importance of routines and homework to a woman who's high as a kite.

He comes up to me after school on Friday, those eyes stare up with sorrow and he asks, "Mr. J., will you be my dad tomorrow?"

Jaydon Breaks Down

"Why you crying, buddy?"

"I'm hungry. Real hungry."

They say you can't take the kids with you; you need to create some space for yourself. You can't adopt them, but they remain a part of you. I teach my class and look over and Jaydon is sobbing, tears running down his face, head in his hands. I know Jaydon probably didn't eat last night. He's told me the stories, they're in a new group home. Mom is on the verge of another nervous breakdown, telling him in the middle of the night to "roll over, go to sleep, honey. There's nothing tonight."

It's hard for me to enjoy a regular meal now, my meal of privilege. I understand food now on a primal level. I see the eyes of my kids. Being able to eat seems like opulence. Guilt comes when I have what I want to eat. I get to sleep at night. I say a prayer for the kids I imagine are without food. Prayers are not feeding them tonight.

They Own These Halls #1

They walk the halls like they own the place. I should say, they walk the halls and *do* own this place. The teacher has sent them out and they're fine with that. These kids don't care for your reading and math anyway. They have their own routines and patterns; all day they are up and down the halls. Their little pack is always on the move, picking up stragglers along the way.

They want it this way. They act out in class to get out. They pick at one another because they can't do the work. They'll mess with the teacher, slap other kids, refuse work, disrupt the whole class: bring the teacher to the boiling point until she screams in frustration, "Get out! You gotta go! Get Out!" If anyone asks, the kids now have their excuse: "She put me out."

They walk the halls, revel in the sounds of their own echoes. They are kings of the palace, no one telling them they can't read or how "below basic" they are. Their hallways are vast canyons, a wondrous playground, the stairwell railings are slides, they never know what's around the next corner. Unity, Movell, Jasmine, Darnell, the crew, logging miles and miles.

They know the nooks and crannies, just keep on moving the whole school day. Make the rounds and then make the rounds again, looking for action, any action to break the tedium. On and on they trudge and laugh and jostle and throw things and knock on doors and pick up and pocket any scrap lying around. They know where the cameras are and they play their cat and mouse game with the security guard, who by lunchtime, has given up on finding them. The teachers are glad to have them gone, have order restored, happy to have their rooms back to themselves and the kids who want to learn. As the day nears an end, they make plans for the next day. "Maybe we can sneak in and play games in the computer lab?" A bargain made, an education lost, and hallways still to roam.

They Own These Halls #2

Here I am, standing outside the classroom on our professional development day and, in a flash, I feel the freedom of Movell and his crew of "runners." I understand them. The uninhibited abandon of having the empty school halls before me. No one to answer to, nowhere to go. I did a full circle around the corridors of the old school and then, what the hell, did another round for good measure. "You're not the boss of me," I laugh as I walk proudly and openly past the classrooms full with teachers and routines.

I sing a song, "walking the halls, walking the hall-alls." I realize, as I walk, the power that comes from "not doing," the feeling of open spaces. Just like Movell, I stride through the halls unshackled; I don't have to obey a bunch of stuff I don't understand. I don't have to face the stress of pretending I know things that I don't! Whatever nonsense those teachers are talking can wait. Here, I have abandon, I have potency. Here, I am not diminished, lacking, wanting. I have found my agency: it's walking these halls. Living moment to moment, I feel the rush of doing something wrong: rebelling, protesting. I will not sit where I don't belong. I will not stay in a class where that teacher hates me! She sees me as a problem. I'm not a problem! I will create my own world here in the halls and the stairwells. I have my crew. I have my world here, my own powerful world!

Shoes

Shoes are controllable. Shoes are understandable. Shoes make sense. Shoes shine. Those who can afford the right type of shoes look "fly." I had okay shoes, but when push came to shove and the kids really wanted to insult me, they would not come after me, they'd go after my shoes. "Mr. J.! Where'd you get those old man shoes? Payless?" Shoes will make a kid watch from the sidelines during a recess football game, so they don't get them dirty. Shoes will make a kid fight to the death. You don't mess with these kids' shoes. A solution to eradicate the feeling that you're nothing, not worth a damn thing. A way of being "all that." Shoes bring worthiness, attention, acceptance. The teachers moan, "If only we could make them care as much about books as they do about their shoes."

Books From the Church

My wife has set up a book drive at our church, which had an overwhelming response. The kids' books came in droves, of all shapes and sizes. At the end of each day, I'd invite the kids to choose the books they wanted. It was a pleasure to see their wonder and amazement at all the different choices. I'd set aside time for the students to free read. I wanted them to experience the pure joy of sitting on the rug and reading. The tension in the room drifted away as the children pored over their very own books, with three or four other books by their side to give to their siblings. "You can create a home library," I encouraged. I felt the sacredness contained in books, true portals to repose and reflection.

When I asked who has books in their home, three hands go up. The kids are not used to having books around, not used to picking up a book and reading. One day, when it was time to pick out books again, Trayzon came up to me sadly, and said, "Mr. J., my mom said I can't bring home any more books. She doesn't know where to put them all."

Hollow

This morning, Janessa passed me in the hall with hollow eyes.
    Eyes so vacant I was afraid to ask,
    "What happened last night?"

Truer than True

    "Happy now, sad later."
    A new song for the kids.
    They catch the dark humor
    and sing along: "Happy now, sad later."

    Trouble is waiting.
    Trouble is everywhere.
    Keep it clean.

Stay on the good foot.
Step over the line, it's
"Happy now, sad later."

Model of Resolve

Latanya comes into class wearing big goofy glasses, an awkward fitting school uniform. Tall and lanky, she takes her place at her desk. A few of the boys are cutting up. She pulls out her pencil. Two girls roll their eyes at each other. She pulls out her notebook. A child runs down the hall laughing outside the room. She focuses on the teacher. Someone throws a paper wad over her head. She takes down her first notes.

Though she seems a perfect target for a bully, the kids leave Latanya alone. She's on grade level for reading and math. Her modeling of what it means to be a good student is her armor. An inherent respect follows her through her day.

Way Too Grown

Chamika wants the boys' attention. She licks her hand and looks them right in the eye. Chamika's already banned from the rec center for having sex in the bathroom.

Chamika will not wear the school uniform. Today, a tight pink shirt shouts "Night Life." She gives lip back to anyone and everyone, knows how to duke it out. Fists up, she circles like an old-school boxer. Shares phone photos of herself giving the world the finger. Chamika has put on weight, she rubs her belly, wants everyone to think she's pregnant. What's Ms. Bluette to do?

"Girl, sweetie child, you're only ten. You're actin' way too grown! Sit down and learn something from the old heads."

Kalil's Love

Kalil came from a brood of ten kids; they would stand next to their aunt at the end of the day on the front porch to get the update on Kalil's day. Like little Russian nesting dolls, they stood in a line and waited to hear the rowdy tales of Kalil's day. The littlest one on the end, all bobbles and bright eyes, looked up at me and said, "Kalil bad."

Kalil loved like no one in the school. He loved with the intensity of a forsaken character in an Italian opera. A tear-your-heart-out, writhing-on-the-floor, desperate kind of love. Who he loved was Kayshawn. And like many a star-crossed lover, none of it was good for him. Kayshawn was wiser in all ways. He would set Kalil up to get him to do his dirty work. Kayshawn knew how to play Kalil just right and Kalil, in the earnestness of his love for Kayshawn, would do what Kayshawn willed. This involved lying to teachers and stealing food for Kayshawn and rifling through teachers' drawers for anything that he could get his hands on. Kayshawn would observe the room with the eyes of a hawk, then set Kalil loose to do his dirty work.

Kayshawn also played with Kalil's affection and would be friendly to others to intentionally exclude Kalil. To purposefully inflict pain on Kalil, to see just how far he could push him without losing him all together. It was a perverse game. Kalil would wail his tears, turn over tables, throw chairs, tear up the room, tear at his breast, all of it for Kayshawn. The depths of Kalil's love would ripple through his body and erupt in the lonely wail of an outcast wolf, howling for a connection with someone, anyone.

Types of Intelligence

"Street smarts," they call it. They should call it street vision or super-vision. A hyper-awareness of your surroundings. A wild-eyed, never resting, tuned-in mentality to jump on any opportunity and not give anyone else the chance to jump on you. Your senses are turned on and tuned in, not to school or education, but to what might harm you, what might destroy you, what might kill you. To survive you need to know what's the "word on the street," because that's where you spend most of your time. Out in the open, open to anything and anyone, you need to know beforehand what might be coming at you,

who has a beef with who. You need to know who carries a gun,
what side to take, where to hide, where to be and not be, how
to keep alive. You do this by keeping your ear to the ground and
knowing "what's up."

Teachers can't measure this by our standards of education. I
capture some of it when I test my kids and they score off-the-
charts high at retelling an oral story. A child will test third grade
in reading and then test college level in retelling a story. There
is such a disparity in the scores, I thought I was doing the test
incorrectly and had to get the results confirmed by the school
psychologist.

These children inhabit an oral culture, you need to be tuned
in, need to know when to watch out. Books don't hold the same
importance or immediate appeal. Why would they? Reading a
book is a luxury. You must tune out from the world around you,
leave this immediate world. You might put yourself in danger.
You need to know what's going on. A book is detached from
the primal physical world; knowledge and education provide
delayed gratification. No chance for reflection. You need to
know how and when to react to the next threat. No place to
read a book. No place to hide. No place to rest.

A Switch Was Flipped

Matthew came to my class in October. He was one of the Charter school kids who had been kicked out for behavioral issues.
One of the physical boys who couldn't ignore a good tussle and
was forever pushing and slapping other kids. Matthew was also
a good conversationalist and would look you right in the eye as
he told you about his love of sports, his siblings, and food.

We sat down to do our reading and I asked Matthew to
read the passage. He started by giving me an overview of what
the pictures in the book meant. I thanked him and then asked
him to actually read the passage, the words. "I just did," he
answered. I realized he had used his intelligence to compensate
for his lack of phonemic awareness. Matthew pieced together

stories by discerning characters, action, and plot through whatever pictures were available.

I immediately tested his reading skills and found he could only read four words per minute. "All right, Matthew, now we know what we need to do. Let's link these letters with sounds, let's chunk it out." Matthew enthusiastically embraced his new understanding. He no longer had to hide and act out to avoid being called on to read. We read together every day. I gave him books to take home and he would report back on how much how he read with his sister. He was excited to show me his progress. Any time he saw me having a spare moment, he would ask, "Mr. J., can we read?" or "Can I come see you at lunch?"

By the end of the year, Matthew was up to ninety-four words per minute and well on his way to being on grade level.

"Doctor" Bernard Smith

They call Bernard my mini-me. He follows me around the halls into my class, leaves his class to come down and see me, say hi. He's very low in reading and math and needs tons of intervention. When I start pulling back the layers, I find out that Mom's dealing drugs out of the house; Mom and Dad are fighting over where he gets to stay. Dad is supposedly born again and talks the talk, although he shows up for the teacher's conference high as a kite. Bernard smiles when he sees me and I'm glad I can be there for him. He's taken to signing his papers "Doctor" Bernard Smith, which is a chuckle for us and a belly laugh for the teachers. But Bernard is proud in his own way and plods on despite the obstacles.

It's reading time and the administration insists that the students read complex text, so I drag the kids kicking and screaming into a nineteenth-century text, a historical memoir written by Lewis and Clark. Pure torture for everyone. A full-out rebellion erupts and who can blame them? The ones who can read struggle through, some who can't put on a good show and pretend to read. The kids who can't read at grade level resist by tearing up the text, running out of the room, throwing pencils. Bernard comes up to my desk with his paper, looks me in the eye, and says, "I don't know."

"All right, start by circling the words you don't understand."

Bernard goes back to his desk for a minute, then comes back and hands me his paper. The whole text is circled.

The Wild Boys

Some boys are so active, wild, and vocal, they get marginalized early. These boys have a hard time sitting still, and are usually behind in their reading and math. They cut up and lose precious days, then months, then years of instruction and learning. They get suspended, put out of the room to wander the halls.

Most teachers don't understand them, will yell at them, "Boy! Go sit over there in the corner and shut your mouth." Or right up in their face: "Little boy, do you hear me? Sit still!" And so on, until the boys get the message. They look at the clock and pine mightily for lunch and recess when they can cut loose. They get to run and tackle and fight and talk junk and be as loud and rough as they like. Then they must head back in, herded into straight lines and barked at like little prisoners tied to a world where they know they don't belong. Back in class and: "Sit your self down!" They get it and take it for as long as they can. They understand the teacher does not want them around. They start messing up more to get sent out. Roam the halls and then the streets. Eventually, don't bother going to school at all. Who cares? Teachers breathe a sigh of relief and are happy when they don't show up. Who will know? Nobody. Lost boys. Lost souls and lost early.

Kaydo and the Peanut Butter and Jelly Sandwiches

I start our Monday morning lesson and see Kaydo head down on his desk, sobbing. I get the other kids going on their task and pull him outside. "What's up, Kaydo?" I'm hoping it's not about his beatings, which it usually is.

He holds his stomach and bends over in pain. "I haven't eaten since Friday."

I ask my paraprofessional to please go get him something from the cafeteria and tell him to hold on a little longer.

Kaydo will break down at any minute, but he always tries to fight through and show a smile. You can't feel what that hunger feels like. It's not the luxury of fasting for cleansing. It's a kind of slow torture; a deep ache. They say his dad sings outside of the Safeway for money. Supposedly he's pretty good, when he's not high. The singing is a diversion, so his wife can go in and steal some food. I've seen the parents weaving up the sidewalk, stoned out of their minds on crack, making their wayward way to school to pick up their three kids.

The weekend is a long time to go without free school meals. My wife started making Kaydo some peanut butter and jelly sandwiches in a brown bag for him to take home on Fridays. As the final bell rings, Kaydo clutches the sack like a treasure. He sees his parents and quickly hides his stash of sandwiches deep inside his book bag, then walks hesitantly up the street to meet them.

Friday, When the Last Bell Rings

They don't want to go. The worst kids, the ones that gave you hell all week long, dawdle. They don't want to go home to their real hell. Everyone here tries hard to remember that each child is giving their best, offering all they have that day. But now, it's time to go, teachers and staff are exhausted, ready to take a deep breath and rest over the weekend. But these children don't want to leave, they'll hide, run down to the computer room, disappear into the halls, some even sneak into the closets. They hang around the corners of your room. As much pain as this school brings them, it's still way better than what they face at home. They pretend not to hear you say, "Roll out, time to roll." Still, they linger.

Jewel's Graduation

The countdown had started for the big day. Most of the other kids were getting hyped about graduation day. Jewel was anxious. Everyone knew her mom was hanging out at the corner by the 7-11, selling her body for crack. Jewel would change her route to school to not have to walk by her mom. The kids would tease Jewel hard when they felt like it. "Hey, girl, saw your crackhead mom out there this morning looking all crazy."

Jewel worried about the graduation clothes. What will I wear? She worried about the questions. Why isn't your mom here? Jewel worried about sitting alone after the ceremony while everyone else was eating cake with their family and friends. She worried about no one taking photos, no one taking her out for a fun meal after the celebration. But what terrified Jewel the most was that her mom might actually show up.

3

THE JOB

This Job

This job will get you, smack you down, make you cry, make you beg the kids for mercy. The sheer intensity takes its toll. In-your-face from the moment you walk in the door.

The school year—a long, drawn-out baseball season, a marathon, not a sprint. The job makes you feel inadequate. You have to learn how to lose. You can't "mail" this in. The maladies keep coming: headaches, indigestion, chest pains, chronic coughs, colds, flu, bronchitis; leg, wrist, elbow, foot, and knee injuries.

Take a day off to pull yourself together, the administration is on your back, threatening your job. You're trapped: pressure from above, pressure from below, caught in this purgatory, losing years off your life.

Teachers leave in droves. Some hold it together on pins and needles; others take a long, slow descent into sleepless nights and tortuous, thankless days.

Literacy Warrior

I call her the "literacy warrior," and Ms. Bluette dresses the part, wearing her flowery bandanas with colorful dresses draping her curvy frame. She has risen from nothing, poor as Eastern Shore Maryland dirt poor. When she was ten years old, she watched her dad get pulled out to sea and drowned. As a single mom, she worked in the chicken processing plants of Frank Perdue to raise her kids, then cleaned houses with her teenage daughters. She went back to school and got her teaching degree, then a master's degree and planted herself here at Amidon. She was the family's matriarch, and no one, I mean no one, was going to take this job from her. She endured the Rhee Invasion and five principals in ten years. Pointing to our new principal, she would say, "That lady there? Shiiii-it, I'll be here long after she's gone." She was paying for her granddaughter's college education, driving a nice sedan, and nothing was rooting her out.

Walking past her room, you'd hear shouts, "Sit down, little boy!" as she gave her lesson on figurative language and the wonders of simile and metaphor. She understood the deep value of education. She had been lifted up from nothing through learning, desire, and grit. She loved the nuances of words and truly wanted to help the kids learn and grow. Everyone had to come to some bargain with these children, some way of getting through to them and surviving the day. Being straight-up tough and relentless was her way.

She told the story of how one year a "little boy," Dayvon, would not sit still, was flat out crazy: she kept him tucked in behind her desk. Every time he moved, she'd say, "Hey! Get back in there!" And there he'd sit, behind the desk. "He actually learned a bit," she said. "Extreme kids? Extreme measures. You think these are regular kids? Think again," she would say, and "You going to let a ten-year-old take away your good job?" And with that resolve, she'd plow through the day, laying it on the line, as tough as they come, giving no quarter, and getting the job done year after year. "But this job," she would say, "this job seeps in, gets into your pores. These kids? I mean, it's just crazy." She had trouble sleeping, was tormented by a recurrent dream that little Dayvon had come out from behind her desk and had stolen her prized Lexus from the parking lot. He was speeding away down Fourth Street. She yelled out to him as he laughed his crazy laugh and drove off into the darkness.

Poppin'

"We gonna get 'em poppin' today, Mr. J.?" Ms. Bluette greeted me as I entered her room. She was referring to our term for keeping the kids engaged during our vocabulary lessons. When the big change in staff occurred, Ms. Bluette took advantage of the overall confusion and had me working primarily with her. With all the uncertainty, I was glad to be taken under her generous wing.

We hit it off right from the start. Co-teaching, we challenged each other to keep our commitment to the kids and their learning, no matter the obstacles. I provided technical know-how and used my experience of teaching creative writing and coaching basketball. Ms. Bluette provided her wide knowledge that came from teaching and surviving in DC for the last ten years. She also knew the kids inside and out and how to motivate them.

Technically, I was the special education (SPED) teacher, and she was the general education teacher. We both threw aside these labels and pitched in together to ensure all the kids were getting and giving their best. Sometimes I worked with the SPED students and sometimes Ms. Bluette did. Whatever was best in that moment, that's what came to the front. The students responded. Throughout the first semester, reading scores for the kids went up. When the students were having behavior issues, we both pitched in to put out the fires. True teamwork. Some of the students even thought we were married. A model of how co-teaching can work: when teachers are selflessly committed to the children and the SPED students are being adequately served, everyone benefits.

Unfortunately, this partnership was short-lived. Due to staffing changes and shortages, the administration decided my services were needed elsewhere. As the SPED students went back to receiving scattered and inconsistent services, the progress of the class hit the skids.

Whew

"Whew, Mr. J., just whew." Ms. Taylor is our one social worker for our 380 kids. This is her "not enough hours in it" day. "Where do I start?" Ms. Taylor asks. "With the parents? With the kids? With the administration? With Central Office?"

"Coming and going, Mr. J." Parents are on her back, yelling at her out on the street for her trying to hold them accountable, for contacting social services, telling folks about the beatings they give the kids, the drugs they're selling out of their homes. At the end of the day, "Who's watching? Who's accountable for these kids?"

Up and down the halls, her name called again over the intercom, Ms. Taylor off to put out another fire, shaking her head: "Whew."

Crabs In a Pot

"Why can't y'all just get along, help each other?" Ms. Bluette pleads. "You're acting like crabs in a pot. You ever see crabs in a pot? One tries to escape, and the others drag it right back down. Right to the bottom. You like the bottom? Help each other out, please, children, help each other. Don't be like crabs in pot!"

Reading the Story of Ruby

It's late September and the swelter of Indian summer permeates the stagnant air. The kids have come in from recess and the classroom is funky with sweat. My time to read aloud, to settle the kids in. I pull out *The Story of Ruby Bridges*. I am smack dab in the middle of thirty-two fifth graders crammed into the too-small room. Children everywhere. I ask the kids if anyone has heard about Ruby Bridges, and no one responds. I show the kids the cover of the book, with little Ruby dressed up for her first day of school.

As I read on about her struggles and courage in the face of white hatred, I start to sweat a bit. I look over the faces and see them rapt with attention. They want to know what's going to happen to their little Ruby. I show the kids the illustrated pictures of angry white adults with contorted ugly faces berating a little Black girl dressed up like she's going to church, as she crosses the lines of segregation. My students and I can imagine the vitriol spewing out of the white folks' mouths.

A central mystery of the teaching profession is you often don't know what your students are thinking, but right now I have a pretty good idea. I had dissolved in many ways from being "that white man," to "Mr. J.," and over time, when you're with the kids all day, you become their "teacher." Some of the racial barriers melt away by our pure humanness, by relating to one another so personally every day. I am in an in-between place, not one of them, but with them, supporting them, listening to them. I glance up and see the clear eyes following me and the pictures of white adults that look like me, except they have clenched fists, mean mouths, angry bodies. They are menacing the sweet, proud, vulnerable Ruby as she walks to school.

I don't stop or editorialize. I plow through the text. By story's end, we see how a little girl showed the way, tore down the walls of ignorance, and carved a path. We see that a child can be a courageous leader. There's a long silence. I am lost. How do I lead the discussion? I'm disgusted, rattled, and ashamed of what I've shared. I knew about racism but to see it projected and thrown at little Ruby Bridges is a lightning jolt. My stomach is sick. I have to hold on. The kids wait, are all settled in with their brown eyes beamed in on me. I ask for questions. Leah, the bright light who has worked with me to dramatically improve her reading, raises her hand. With a concerned and confused face, she asked me, "Mr. J., do you like Black people? Is you racist?" I didn't know how to respond. I was speechless. I had never explored the depths of hatred so intimately as when reading about it with these precious children, my students, who I practically live with every day. They waited for a response. I shook my head and with a low, grave voice answered, "No, I hope not, sweetheart. No."

Chalk Smoke

"All right, y'all. I want to see some chalk smoke. Now!" I exhorted the students. They knew this was their signal to start writing. "Chalk smoke" was our inside joke about all the smoke fuming off their busy pencils.

Pencil on paper has innumerable benefits. Kinesthetically there's a flow that occurs, a connection when a child starts the physical process of writing. No longer distracted, students concentrate and express themselves. Plus, they have the satisfaction of seeing the work they produce right in front of them on the page.

"I see Darnell has some chalk smoke going. What about you, Calvin?" Writing is contagious. Across the room, Darnell calls back, "Chalk smoke, Mr. J.! See it?"

Ms. Bluette's Lament

"Mr. J., what are we gonna do with these kids? They keep throwing us this and that and coming up with new principals and new plans, but who's gonna worry about these kids? Who's going to take care of what they need? All these adults just worrying about adults. This is not a game!"

Portrait of a Principal

I arrived at my one o'clock meeting with the principal and was shocked. She sat in her office with a stunned look on her face. I asked, "This is what she did?"

Ms. Hilton had the look of someone who had just witnessed a disaster. And she had. Katrisha had a psychotic meltdown. A hurricane, a tornado had swept through her office. Little first-grade Katrisha had gone off, torn the room to shreds. The whole room had been blown up, torn paper was scattered all over the floor, nothing was left hanging on the walls, chairs were broken, tables tossed over.

"Should we still meet?" I asked.

Her face was flushed, eyes wet.

"Sure," she said, "we need to talk," and out of the rubble, she picked up a chair.

"My Babies"

"My babies are gonna to be all right."

"My babies did this today."

The teachers use this term of endearment when talking

about the kids. This spark, this flame, this is what brought them to teaching in the first place. This phrase conveys their deep love for their students, a recognition of the children's intrinsic value, of the teachers' humanity and decency, all of which lies beneath the squabbling and incessant testing.

Left Behind

Ms. Alton came from the old school way of treating special education (SPED) kids as special, as kids needing extra love and tenderness more than rigorous instruction. She had a real way with the "lower" children, the ones who struggled mightily with their reading and math. She had flowers in her room and stuffed toys and crayons and coloring books. She would burn incense and play meditation music. Ms. Alton had the kids sing songs and dance. She'd have special treats and surprises when they tried their best or helped each other out. Her motto was, "Every child is special and my kids are really special." This is what she knew about doing her job and the kids loved her like a mom.

She would lead them down the halls, singing, and they would follow her like little ducklings—smiling, clapping, humming. She was home to them, a home full of peace and laughter. She knew nothing of the new instructional strategies and Common Core and how each child was supposed to receive the same education, regardless of aptitude, since No Child Left Behind became law.

This old style of dealing with SPED kids was now thought of as enabling "learned helplessness." There were many women like Ms. Alton in DCPS, women who loved the kids and focused more on their significant social-emotional needs than strict education. Some teachers fought the big changes and were removed quickly; others, like Ms. Alton, paid lip service to it and would revert to old ways when no one was looking. She never really understood what the administration was looking for and had no interest in changing how she taught the kids.

Push came to shove when teachers were required to keep hard data on the growth of their students. This involved a solid understanding of technology and using Excel spreadsheets. Ms. Alton had a hard time navigating a computer, let alone processing student growth data. Well into her fifties now, she needed this job. She supported her family: the job provided them with income and decent healthcare. Her husband had a chronic illness and couldn't work.

Finally, after too many poor scores on her observations, she was "IMPACTed" out for reasons that she really didn't understand. After twenty years at Amidon, she cried on my shoulder. "What am I going to do?" I had no answers and patted her back.

After she left, her "brood" of SPED kids were lost. They no longer had their smiling, singing advocate and protector.

Learning to Breathe

"Everybody take a breath."

A funny idea, right? "We already are breathing, Mr. J!"

Pausing to take deep breaths with the kids has been a lifesaver. Children who know they lack the wherewithal to hold it together, learn to realize breathing can help them. This world moves very fast, and the kids like to speed it up to warp speed. Having a regular breathing practice helps students slow it all down, feel their feet, and get some learning and work done. Doing deep breaths before every class starts and before and after transitions helps settle all of us, me included.

De'Wayne was the most troubled kid I had met. He was as raw as they come. He could barely read and had a hard time remembering two plus two. "Drug baby," people said. He had a wild eye, was a chronic hall runner, always looking to escape something. Breathing had helped him begin to function as a student in class. He knew that it helped him.

This was a big day, the assistant principal's announced observation of my class. I had made a bargain to keep De'Wayne and the other kids in line. The prize for making today's observation successful was a pizza party.

The observation was about to begin, and I told the kids, "All right, let's start with our deep breaths. We all want pizza, right? Okay, let's do ten deep breaths."

De'Wayne piped up. "Can we do thirty?"

Southwest Projector Screen

No screen to show the video. I prop up a big piece of cardboard and get a student to stand on each side and hold the ends. Ms. Finch, the music teacher, pops in. "What on earth are you doing? Y'all is soooo ghetto! Oh my god!" and laughs out the door and down the hall.

Pimpin' Out the Kids

That's what Ms. Bluette called it. They swoop in, the celebrities, the basketball stars, the politicians, the superstars of educational reform. Kareem Abdul-Jabbar! Joel Osteen! The mayor! The school on high alert, the "trouble" kids tucked out of sight in far-away rooms. The worst ones were told they really didn't have to come to school that day if they didn't want to. A big show. A news' flash. Feed the people a feel-good story about the high poverty kids. "They're so cute, aren't they?"

At such events, the kids do put out some great smiles. They are overjoyed to get the attention. Enthralled by the bright lights, they brighten and their radiant faces shine. The kids will gather in the library, some star will read them a story, hopefully no one will "kirk out" or say something ridiculous or profane, there will be hugs and smiles, the principal will be in the photo ops, and then, the stars will be on their way. Nothing really changed, just a diversion, throw the kids a few crumbs, make everyone feel better. Everyone except for the kids, left once again to figure out an inconstant world and fight for their own survival.

In the Afternoon, We Do Fool

Ms. Bluette says, "In the morning we do school; in the after-noon, we do fool." The kids try their best to hold it together all morning and then that pent-up energy busts loose on the playground and in the lunchroom. Fights, cursing, crying, melt-downs, it comes in waves during the noon hour. A morning spent growing grit, of conforming, of staring at words and equations; it boils over. After the confusion and mayhem of the break, it's time to get back to class, to restore order. I look out at the class and see everyone moving, everyone in motion, tapping, talking, jostling, shaking, crying, yelling. I think this must be the result of the stress of generations of slavery, of Jim Crow, of segregation, of corrections systems, jails, guns, drugs, and hatred lingering and passed on. This intense stress handed down from generation to generation. Hopelessness and fear. This is the slow drip of racism. They call it PTSD, but here it runs even deeper. It's outside and inside, a cruel and relent-less pressure of not being good enough, of not succeeding, of being a cast out. We expect a curiosity for learning to magically spring from this turbulent terrain filled with imminent, real, and embedded danger. We are the fools.

Below Basic

Here in DCPS, there are four labels, and everyone knows them: advanced, proficient, basic, and below basic. A labeling system based on standardized tests that groups the students, who learn to see themselves through this lens, who know themselves and their capabilities by what group they're in and who's in their group.

I walk past Ms. Jackson's room and can hear she's had enough. She erupts in her southern drawl: "You all are sooooo below basic!" Her voice escalates and rattles around the room. "Do you know what that means, Traevon? Do you? It means you ain't going nowhere! It means you will always be a little ghetto rat! You know why? Because all you want to do is play, play, play. Do you want to learn to read? Do you want to sit still? Do you want to listen? Do you? Mr. Below Basic! Y'all is an embarrassment to your race. You all are low, low, low, low down! All you is below, below, below basic!"

School Rules

The kids keep pushing her today. They won't sit still, won't listen, and keep on whining about this and that. Ms. Bluette's had it. "Boy, you think this is Burger King? This is school! You can't have it your way!"

Bags of Shavings

I start the lesson, hear this scratching sound. I stop, it stops. I start teaching again, the sound starts again.

I walk around the class and see shavings, eraser shavings, piles of them in the pencil bins.

"What's up with that?" I ask Lamont.

He points to the pile of shavings in his desk. "That? Ms. Moore let us do this last year. It relaxes us."

Ms. Sampson on Classroom Management

"My first job, the principal said: 'I come in here and the kids are running around out of control, I'll take over and show you how it's done. I come in a second time and have to take over, you're gone.'"

With her glasses and lithe frame, Ms. Sampson looks like a hawk. She keeps the students on a tight leash, barks at the wild boys to "Sit down, little boys!" Gets right up in their face and says, "Do you want to meet the Wicked Witch? Do you?"

And when they ramp it up, she lays down the truth: "I will kick out all these windows before you take my good government job!"

Ms. Brown's Bargain

It keeps her up nights, but she had a decision to make. A decision to survive. She has finally given up on the half of the class that is running her ragged—the half that's not receiving their allotted special education hours, that needs the small group, that needs specialized instruction, that needs to be out of her hair! She has her group around her, the ten or so kids that want to learn and she reads with them, gives them their assignments. The others are grouped in the back of the room, clustered around computers, playing video games; anything to stupefy the kids and keep them from tearing her room apart. This is her devil's bargain. She's not proud of it, but it might get her through the year until she can get the hell out of here.

Promises of What? What Are We Promising?

I'm not sure what the focus of this "education" is? Is the goal for the kids to be free thinkers? Radicals on the fringe questioning everything and everyone? To be civil rights leaders? Activists? To be good worker bees ready for the cubicle farms of tomorrow? There is an underlying premise that the white world has it better and that somehow these children should strive to embrace that reality. What is confusing to me must be confusing to them. Their inner intelligence tells them something is wrong even if they can't put a finger on it. How can you get the kids to "intrinsically" believe in education with vague promises of being ready for the corporate world or going to college, whatever that might mean?

In 2008, the whole work world shifted. After the great recession, much of the "white world" was left in shambles with foreclosures, bankruptcies, and millions without jobs. If we are to prepare these children for the future, we need to teach them to communicate, think, and be adaptable to an ever-shifting reality. Flexibility and education are key because the new world does not offer any tangible stability, imagined or not.

Don't Dare Get Sick

Time and again, the administration will stress how you should never take any time off; how when you do take leave, you are putting an enormous strain on your colleagues and the school. They rarely talk about a teacher's health. The school will fall into an all-out panic when a steady teacher needs a sick day. A teacher being out of the building often leads to a total collapse of their classroom, which then has a domino effect throughout the whole hall. When you're gone, the kids tear it up. Kids run in and out of classrooms, fight, and generally tear the school apart.

Children that have such little order and so little trust in their day-to-day reality are thrown into disarray at any shift in schedule. Trust and respect are earned through the consistency of their teacher's kindness and presence. They will not trust any substitute. The teacher is caught in the crosshairs. Any teacher who does take off for health reasons knows they will return to an administration that is questioning their integrity, a torn-up classroom, and a bunch of kids that need a few days of intense classroom management to bring them back into focus.

Can't Get a Substitute

The school has a serious reputation. They call it "The Rock." No substitute teachers will sign up. Kids call the subs "fresh meat." One rolled out at lunch, left a note: *Had to leave for my secret agent assignment.*

Another sub had a novel approach. Before the students arrived for class, he scrawled on the whiteboard in big black letters: *Don't Mess With Me!*

Schoolwide Behavior Intervention Plan

It's come down from Central Office. We need more behavior intervention in our school. We teachers look at each other in disbelief. "No kidding, really?" We have one social worker and a school psychologist who is overloaded with testing responsibilities. Who will this new plan fall on? The teachers! Here we go. Each teacher will provide the names of at least three kids that we believe need to be put on a behavioral plan. How this will be monitored and sustained remains to be seen. When completed, this evaluation phase identifies more than 150 kids out of 380 schoolwide that definitely need some sort of behavior plan.

We know this. Everyone knows this. We teachers know what plans "could" be in place, but there are not enough hands on deck to implement a plan. When a class is overflowing with behavior problems and you lack the proper resources, the best you can hope for is a Band-Aid solution. We draw up the 150-plus behavior plans, go through numerous discussions and enter endless reams of data into online databases. On day one, we watch the whole plan fall apart. Kids rip up their behavior plans, say, "Naw! Hell, no!" when their goals are discussed and generally resist change with every fiber of their being. Time is not built into a teacher's already overloaded schedule to complete more forms. The kids stand around waiting for the teacher to fill out the behavior forms at the end of class: a recipe for disaster. When the kids mill around, they get restless. When they get restless, they start pushing each other or pulling each other or kicking each other or grabbing shirts and hair. You need to keep things tight, keep things moving.

This chaos lasts for two weeks until the whole issue slips away. Once again, a grand plan was initiated without practical considerations and resources. This increases the general sense of exhaustion and cynicism throughout the building. The kids are once again presented with an inconstant, shifting reality, while the teachers are given yet another unrealistic task with crazy expectations, lacking enough support or follow through. The cynicism becomes entrenched, so that any new initiative becomes something to endure rather than something to embrace. Teachers, like the kids, want to have a chance to succeed, have plans that they can actually implement. A culture of waiting out each new idea arises as the next idea comes down the pike. The main focus for teachers becomes narrowed to trying to survive and keep your job in this *Alice in Wonderland* world of brain-twisting concepts and fanciful plans.

There Is Never Not Something to Do

In some ways, this job is easy. There is no choice but to give to the children. Give to the immediacy of their issues, their problems, their traumas right before your eyes. This job is tangible, fast, and overwhelming. You can either dive in and help or be swept to the side by the rushing current of pain. A fight breaks out, break it up. A child starts crying, console her. A young boy is frustrated with a math problem, help him work it out. Three kids are bullying another one, have a conference. You communicate caring with your body; you communicate caring with your words. You are in the middle of this now; communicate in any manner you can, but keep it positive. There's a simple calculus to helping other human beings. A beauty to this job is that there's always something to do, someone to help. Don't expect anything back, free yourself, dive into the immediacy of "giving."

Feeding off the Energy

Though the job exhausted me mentally and physically, I felt an energy when I walked into the door. A shot of vibrancy and purpose. I found myself smiling and laughing with the kids. I learned their names and would call out, "Hey, Tywaun" and "All right, Keisha" as they shuffled off to class. Lines of kids giving me high fives. It was so alive, so real, so human. I was no longer plugged into a computer all day, no longer lost in space, stuck in the cyberworld, wherever that was. I loved the physicality of the job, the reality of the kids, their lives. *This is real*, I thought. The immediacy of it all resonated with me, and I would lose myself for hours in the everchanging palette, focused on just serving the kids. I was filled with a feeling of service, of giving over, of never not having enough energy to meet the kids where they were at.

The Real Battle

Ms. Bluette leaned over and touched my arm. "What we're doing here, Mr. J., is fighting ignorance. This here is a war against ignorance and hopelessness; we need to teach these kids to read, to think, to hope, or they have no chance. I know where they end up."

Last Day of School

I sit on the stoop watching the kids dissolve into the city. The school year ends abruptly. You run and run and run for months, surrounded by kids, then one day—*Poof!* It all disappears and you're alone again.

It's noontime in June and the swamp-like summer swelter of DC has begun to set in. Ms. Walker walks up and sits next to me. I always admired her teaching expertise, dedication to the kids, sense of humor, and low-key demeanor.

"You helped the boys this year, Mr. J. You really did."

"Maybe some. Hope so. So, you're leaving?"

"Not proud of it, but I have to go, this place gets inside of you." She sighed. "After seven years, I became angry like the kids. It gets inside your blood—the anger, the pain, it eats away at you. I was from the suburbs in California. This world is as strange to me as it is to you."

"Didn't know that."

"Yes, Mr. J., not all of us are from the hood." She tilted her head and we laughed. "I just have to get out. Get away from all this: the administration beating down on you, the crazy expectations for the kids, four different principals, the violence; all that scratching and clawing, for what? What are we doing here? I found myself becoming more and more like this world. It's starting to harm me, my relationships, my spirit. I'm married; I have to treat my husband right. I want to have kids. I'll be teaching over in Northwest where I have a chance. I've done what I could."

4

COLOR LINES

Language Barriers

I sit down to help a girl read. She haltingly starts, then touches my arm. "You're white, aren't you?"

"Yes, honey, I'm white."

"Then how come you don't speak Spanish?"

What Color Am I?

I asked a student to please sit down, and he replied, "I don't listen to white people."

My paraprofessional, Ms. Witt, stepped in, "Look at my arm. Look, boy!" She pointed to her light-skinned arm. "What color is that? Am I Black? Am I white? What color am I? What color are you? Is anybody really all white or all Black? Isn't everybody mixed? What does color have to do with it anyway? People are people. Wake up, son! People are people!"

Choices

Mr. Dean, the assistant principal, strode into the room and read the kids the riot act. "You can't *afford* to waste this time and lose your education. You can't *afford* to not take advantage of your teachers. You have good teachers here. Mr. J. knows his stuff. Ms. Bluette is an educated person. They have college degrees. You do not have any privilege in this world. You have to scrap and claw for anything you can get. If you want anything in this world, you need to get ready to work for it. You have to do more than other people. Take advantage of this opportunity.

You are Black, you are Black kids, do you understand me?" You could hear a pin drop.

"You are not like Mr. J., here. He's white; he has privilege in this world. He can do what he wants." The kids' eyes swept to me sitting in the back of the room and *bam!* the whole argument of white privilege hit me. I did have choices in this world. I did have a good education, opportunities, a good chance to succeed, not a crooked, gamed-up chance like these children. I saw in stark terms the split between our two worlds and how blind someone can be to the magnitude of something—even when it's right in front of your face.

Safety

We were meeting to review Dominic's education and behavioral goals and his mom and dad came into the conference room. Their body language told me they wanted nothing to do with me. I started talking about Dominic's growth in some areas along with his challenges when Mom, Dyani, piped up, "How do you know, Mr. J.? You just sittin' there lookin' angry all the time. I know what you think, you think I'm too young to be having these babies. That I have too many babies. That I can't handle my own children. I know what you white people think." Meanwhile Dad was turned all the way around, just showing me his back and a small sliver of his face. The psychologist, Ms. Nottingham, jumped to my defense. She knew the parents and said, "Look, Dyani, Dominic likes Mr. J.; I see them working together all the time." Mom paused, then looked at her husband. "Dominic did say he likes Mr. J. He did."

I chimed in. "I like Dominic. I love to see his reading go up. He has a great sense of humor. Sure, he's wild sometimes. He pulls it back together."

Mom laughed. "He can be wild, I know. I hear you, Mr. J."

From then on, Mom and Dad were my biggest supporters. We'd meet on the porch after school to discuss Dominic's day.

They needed to know their child was safe, that he was okay with a white man.

Color Lines Blur

I never really knew how high-poverty Black people lived, what they thought, what they had to do to survive. I played basketball my whole life—hoops was my main experience of Black culture. I loved the "cool" side of Black: Earl Monroe was my favorite player growing up. I modeled his moves, singing to myself, "Spin, Pearl, Spin." At sixteen, I was on an all-Black (except for me) summer league team. My nickname was "Smoke," and I proudly wore my jersey with the moniker on the back when I went back to my mostly white high school. As I got older, I played hoops at the tough playgrounds: Candy Cane, Turtle Park, Eastern Market. The players were mostly Black. I'd play for hours and go back home. We lived in the diverse areas of Takoma DC and Takoma Park for ten years. I had volunteered for four years at The Phillips School in Laurel and taught creative writing classes to kids of many colors, economic backgrounds, and nationalities.

Here, it was different; I was submerged within an unfamiliar culture for hours a day. Surrounded by Black adults everywhere I went. Surrounded by Black kids every day. Making home visits, calling parents and grandparents, talking to the people of the neighborhood daily after school on the steps. Over time, the color lines blurred.

Of course, the kids had seen white people before on the TV and on the street, but most of these kids had never known a white person. Many believed I was light skinned. I came to know the parents beyond their saying, "That white man" this and "That white man" that. Most learned to trust me. After a while, some would smile when they saw me, say, "Hey, Mr. J.," and give me some dap or a hug.

White People

We sit around the reading table. I insist that everyone participate.

No one's allowed to opt out.

Breanna barks, "Mr. Jankowski's doing too much. White people do too much."

Bernard, my mini me, pops up from his seat, pounds the table with his fist, "Mr. Jankowski's not white!"

Hair

"Hair is very important to people here. You don't cut these kids' hair," Ms. Bluette told me. Ms. Parker, a white lady, had once cut a girl's hair in school, and Ms. Bluette never forgave her. "You don't do that to a Black person. Black people cut black hair." And I got this: the symbolism of somebody from another race taking something from a Black child; the reality of not having control over your body, your environment, of who defines style or beauty.

I look out at my class. Oh, the styles! The styles! The glorious variations on hair! The bobbles and the bows! A rainbow of colors—a kaleidoscopic array of styles before me. The room fans out like a coral reef full of tropical colored ribbons and bows, hair jutting up at amazing angles, hair braided and falling down backs, hair pulled to one side, few the same as the other, expressiveness and joy in the wide-open infinity of possibility, of unique styles of hair.

Shades of Laughter

I had become more comfortable in front of the class now and was using the students' names. I asked a question and called on Latifa. She responded, "My name's not Latifa, Mr. J. It's Latia."

I was surprised and responded, "You mean I've been calling you Latifa all this time? Get out!" The kids broke into spontaneous laughter, and I busted out laughing too.

After they had settled in, Aaliyah raised her hand. "Mr. J., can you do that again?"

"What? Say, *Get out?*"

"No. No. Laugh and have your face turn all red again. Can you laugh like that again?"

Coming to Terms

Like most days at Amidon, I felt stretched. Like an accident was waiting to happen. Then it did.

Coach was needed somewhere else, and I was left alone with the thirty-plus kids in the afterschool athletic program. I was out on the back field, running the kids through laps and starting to get our football drills together. It was May and summer was already here. The DC humidity was coming in waves and the gym doors were open so the kids could get a drink of water. Suddenly, I heard a wail from inside, "Mr. J.! Mr. J.!" and Javonna came running out from the gym, sobbing. "They stole my backpack! My new backpack!"

"Give me a second, let me get these kids—"

"No! No!" she cried and off she ran.

I couldn't just leave those kids outside unattended so I started the drills. I figured Javonna would come back and I could deal with the backpack after practice.

As practice ended, I turned toward the gym door and saw Javonna's dad, Leon, eyes on fire, storming right at me. Out of nowhere Coach appeared and yelled, "Leon! Slow down! Leon! Get over here!"

Leon had been one of Coach's football players at Anacostia High and he revered and respected him. Leon turned back and went to Coach. I saw him gesturing wildly and could hear him say, "This white man…that white man… He needs to lose his job over this!"

When practice was over, I headed back inside and Coach said, "Don't worry, I got you."

I had a rough night's sleep and came to school the next morning not knowing what was going to happen. As the kids had breakfast, I noticed Leon across the cafeteria looking at me. He looked angry, but Coach came over and told me to go talk with him.

"We found the backpack—" Leon began.

"Good. Sorry 'bout that. I was alone. Had all those other kids to deal with."

Then Leon's whole demeanor shifted. "Look," he said. "I shouldn't come at you like that. Coach tells me you're all right."

I looked him in the eye and said, "Thanks. I appreciate that. I love working with Javonna, you know. Her reading is coming along."

"I know. I know. Thanks. Thanks for what you do."

Code Switch

Ms. Bluette switches when she's with her "sistahs." She drops the "white talk" she learned in college. Free now, she brings it way down, talks real slow, each sound rolls off the tongue, straight from the soul.

Watermelon Man

I find myself barking out, "Sit down, little man!" or "Little girl, whatchyou got going on over there? Fix it!"

Ms. Sampson laughs, calls over to Ms. Bluette, "Look at him. He's like the watermelon man, turning Black right before our eyes."

Ms. Raynes said I was Black like Bill Clinton.

Coach said, "Shit. Five years on The Rock? You're Black now."

I Leave This at Night

After the school day ends, I go back to my predominately white neighborhood, where most people are well off; sure, there are struggles remaining from the Great Recession—houses underwater, people managing a bunch of debt, marriage problems, kids with their troubles. That's a type of fear, but down here at Amidon there's a deeper fear, deep in the corridors of dark thoughts and hopelessness.

I drive home; my neighborhood is a quiet place, with no crime, save the rare occurrence of teenagers ransacking through unlocked cars. I sit and listen to the silence, but the swarm of the day remains, the kids remain. Images of the day flow across my mind. I score myself on what I handled well and what I botched up. How I could have been more compassionate or maybe I needed to be tougher? Then I go through the roster of my kids, imagining them returning to their worlds. I know Jaydon might not be eating tonight, and Kaleeb is probably running the streets; Kalil is bopping around from crisis to crisis, and De'Wayne's getting knocked around because a teacher called home about his behavior. All of this is in me now; I am wider and deeper. I hope my heart won't crack, that I won't crack, that the weight of it won't make me bitter, that I can hold on to some hope.

It's peaceful here at home. I'm not living like my students, with the perpetual anxiety of not knowing what violence the next moment might bring, how it could come tumbling down on their little shoulders; they live with the stress of poverty 24-7 and do not have the luxury of coming and going, of leaving that world. My students are smack in the middle of it since drawing their first breath. It's all they know, and it informs everything they say and do. The kids haunt me. I can see each face as I close my eyes; they come to me in dreams, and it's a heartache I wake with, a transference of their pain and despair. Am I helping anything? Anyone?

5

Music in the Halls

Microwaves

As the pre-K kids pass, they call out, "Hey, Mr. J.," and give me little pinkie waves, "microwaves."

So full of innocence and freedom, wonder and friendliness, trust.

I hope that it will last.

Primary Education

I look and learn. Watch and learn. The teacher is the learner. I go down low to understand. Deep inside. Who can I forgive here? Start with yourself. Open wide. The joy of the children bursts through.

Music in the Halls (These Children Are Music) #1

I walk these halls and hear the music. The children singing in their classrooms. I hear tunes in my head.

The music is everywhere: in the kids' shouting, fighting, clapping, erupting into laughter.

All of it sings to me. The kids are moving like the wind, they are talking with each other, sorting it out, discovering, wondering, creating new worlds.

These children are music.

I hear the beat of their footsteps, as they run down the hall.

Just Kids for Now

It's a bright field trip morning. The kids are free of school, the day is theirs. They clap and laugh. The girls form a circle around Devin, sway together and sing:

"Rockin' robin, tweet tweet

Rockin' robin, tweet tweet

go rockin' robin, cuz you're really gonna rock tonight."

Devin preens and smiles as wide as the sky, dancing in the middle of all that love.

The Best in Southwest

Ms. Finch is a true diva. She leads the school choir and is a star singer and choral director at her church in Shaw. She has been schooled in music, went to a HBCU, and is proud of her heritage. She brings the kids together and makes them feel special. She tells them, "Okay! Now it's your time to shine!"

When they hit the stage, the kids are ready to roll. Ms. Finch doesn't hesitate to sneak in her churchy roots in her song selections. She chooses "Walk on the Water," and the kids sway and swing and raise it to the rafters. They hit that sweet, high, full pitch that runs through your soul. There is a catharsis to music. A freedom. The teachers are so happy to see their babies involved, engaged, and succeeding. The kids are totally in their element. Their parents come to the concerts and love the whole thing: dressing their kids up, taking videos for keepsakes, and feeling part of something.

The arts tear down walls, bring people together. The arts create a shared expressive understanding. The arts are the thing that brings this whole community together, that heals the divides that keep this school from thriving.

New Day

The sunlight sings in from the windows and all is forgotten. The day is fresh. I sing:

"It's a new day, it's a ne-ew day,"

and the kids call back:

"It's a new day, Mr. J. It's a ne-ew day."

Together we bring in the morning:
"The sun is shining, I am a-rising . . ."

Dancing to Everybody's Beat

You know what's inclusive? Music is inclusive. This beat is in-clusive. The big speakers are pulled out and the place is jumping as the beat echoes around the old gym.

The special education kids can keep up with everybody now. Chamika who can't read a lick, Bobby who can't add, Harold with his brittle bones and bottle-rimmed glasses—all are wel-comed, none are bullied, none teased. The children swim in unison—all the kids together doing the Wobble.

Coach and I smile to each other across the gym. Rhythm does this. The heartbeat does this. The fractured student body swoops together, weaves and claps as one, pulling together, whole.

Bright Bobbles

On the young heads
shining in the sun,
bright bobbles,
sparkling rainbows,
oranges, reds, purples, yellows.
All on one bright head!
Bopping to springtime.
Bopping to school.

The Good Grandmas

Throughout the community, many of the grandmothers are the glue; they keep it together. It still surprises me how young these women can be, but they are the rocks of the community. They come to the parent-teacher conferences; they keep a solid watch on their grandkids. They are the ones on the school porch, waiting when the school day is done. The grandmothers know the teachers and come to talk—some every day—about how

their grandchild did that day. They are graceful in acceptance
of their responsibility; wise to the world, they have weathered
many storms and bring an evenness to the temperament of
the school. They will ask about homework, and they give their
grandkids boundaries and consequences for their behavior. The
good grandmas want to help and be involved. They harbor a
deep fear of what can happen to a child without an education.
They know what can happen when a child is sent out to fend
for themselves on these streets.

Queens of Southwest

It is late spring, and school will soon be out. The leaves of the
old oak trees throw a gentle shade on the sidewalk. The Johnson girls, aged sixteen, twenty-two, and thirty-two, push stroll-
ers with little ones at their sides, walking down Fourth Street to
the CVS. The construction workers, on top of the steel girders
of the new office buildings, hoot and howl and throw dollar
bills down to the girls. These ladies don't skip a beat. Their sway
is the coming summer. Their sway is ownership. This is their
home, they are not knocked off stride; they are all the love,
desire, chaos, and death these streets hold. They have seen it all,
heard it all, lived it all, and still, they move with an unhurried
grace. With the sway and rhythm of their hips, they let everyone
know this is *their* home.

Coach "Big Dog"

For thirty years, he was a football coach, basketball coach,
and athletic director at Anacostia High School. He persevered
through some really tough times—the crack epidemic and the
shootings that made Anacostia notorious; he buried twenty of
his players. He also won a number of city championships, and
now was living out his golden years at Amidon Elementary.
The big man is known on the streets of Anacostia as Coach
Big Dog. Things changed, new people came in, white people
wanted to coach, and despite his experience and success, Coach

was shuffled down the line. He needed a job and landed here with the little ones.

It was a surprise to him at first, these little tikes not respecting him, giving him lip. But Coach adjusted. He still uses his well-worn and tested mix of tough love and intimidation and most of the kids fall in line. He's bringing his wisdom and experience to the kids here, winning city championships again. He's won trophies at the Big A; he's doing it now for the kids. I pop in as he's teaching the young ones how to play kickball. Our eyes meet and we share a deep chuckle. "Who knew?" I call out.

"Who knew?" he laughs back.

Joy in the Faces

I see joy in the faces of these little children. Their dark pearl eyes hold hope and I see in each child a need to be loved and understood. They afford me this opportunity to hope for all of humanity, to embrace the many shades of our existence. I see it right in front of me every day, in the line of kids heading to class—they're crying and smiling, clapping and singing, waving and winking. The whole universe is within them and within me.

"T.D." White

I gave Terrell this nickname for his propensity to shake loose from defenders and catch touchdowns during recess. As he blew by the others and hauled in another touchdown, I called out, "T.D. White! T.D. White!" After his chest bumps and celebration, he'd slip a glance over and flash a smile.

Later, Terrell saw me in the hall and asked, "Do you have recess duty again tomorrow?"

Here, She Gets Some Respect

Ms. Bluette clues me in, "That's why she comes up here. This is the only place she feels important."

Ms. Johnson is from the neighborhood and has two children in our school, one in my class. She takes a seat and smiles as the class unfolds. I'm happy to have her. One glare from her at a misbehaving child does a lot more than me, a white man, telling these kids to "settle down, please."

She has AIDS, or so the whispers say, is wasting away, less than ninety pounds. Tales of her past—of stripping and whoring, shooting up—follow her down the hall. Follows her kids, too.

She's clean now and trying to do right by her babies while she can. Her smile is sweet and deeply sad. Class over, she shakes my hand, says, "Thank you so much. You're doing great." Her words, more important to me than a compliment from any of those anonymous "observers" from Central Office.

Ms. Raynes Had the Light

Her smile was light, her face sunshine. She lit up the room. She told me to "Let your light shine, Mr. J. I see it shine."

Our school counselor, Ms. Raynes, wrestled with the hardest cases for a living.

She would help out in my class. She taught me how you can "walk through the valley of the shadow of death" and still keep smiling, keep your light shining.

"But these kids," she would say, "they're horrible, just horrible. What are we going to do with these kids? This will be it for me, my last year," she said. "I'm tired now."

Sitting out Front

I sit down out front in my usual spot on the stairs looking out on I Street. From the start, I want to be here to see the parents, to talk with them, to wave as they walk by, to let them know I am present. I teach here. I work with your child. This is one of my favorite times of the day. Class is done, the kids are vibrant. I feel open to whatever might come.

Beautiful old oaks lined I Street, and their leaves throw shadows on the sidewalk. A dance of shade and light as the children fall into their loose groups and gather up their brothers and sisters and meet their moms or aunties or grandmas to begin the stroll home. I wait there for the stragglers who would plop down next to me, just sharing space and small talk about their day. The ease of it envelops me and, even as I bark at a student who is playing too rough or running through the flowers, the eternity and sweetness of the scene centers me. Little children all over the country are walking home from school. Why is education such a nasty business? Why must we see little children as a burden or at a deficit? Why can't we love these children for who they are?

Demetrius Blesses the Class

I'm called in to help. Demetrius is running around the room, splashing the kids with "holy water."

"I absolve you of your sins! I cast out the evil! Bless you, bless you all! You are absolved from your evil ways!" He runs in wide-eyed circles around his laughing, hysterical flock.

Music in the Halls (These Children Are Music) #2

Songs come to me walking down the hall, in the lunchroom, amid a full room of kids. A deeper understanding has taken over my consciousness. Instantly, a tune will pop into my head—new rhythms, and the children permeate my mind. Little footsteps dissolve into musical notes. A curtain is pulled back. This feeling runs through my bones, that special part of my brain, the undercurrent, the undertone. This music pervades everything and doesn't judge, doesn't ask. I go where the music leads me. Music helps me to understand the kids at a new level. We are together in this—surrounded and lifted by music.

The Playground

Release! Release! Run! Run! Run! The playground is where a kid can be a kid, where they can throw their arms up at the sky yell, "Yeaaaaa!" and run with the wind. The playground is the center of release—release from the tensions of holding it together for the morning; release from the slights piling up on the kids' shoulders.

The bell rings and kids spill out of the building, running, yelling, and jumping into the air. Balls are torn out of the bags and games immediately commence. The diversity and intensity of activity can't be contained. The "touch" football game deteriorates into a bruising game of tackle. The beefs from the morning start to be settled. The tears of those ignored or dissed by their friend run down cheeks. The cliques, the singing, the jumping rope, and the rock throwing; the packs of little girls stomping around, arguing, snapping their fingers, clapping, "No! No! No! Just No! Danasia!"

Some run to daylight, run and run in circles and don't stop running. The lid kept on in the morning is gone and the pent-up energy explodes. A massive catharsis of joy, despair, and everything in between opens up to the sky of Southwest.

When Coach blows his whistle, it's time to go back in. There are always the five or six boys who want to fight and knock each other around and steal each other's shoes and throw those shoes over the fence out into the city street and curse and call each other Bs. They would rather cuss and fight than go back inside and try to sit still for the whole afternoon.

Graduation Day

Like a dysfunctional family pulling it together for a big wedding, the ghosts permeating the school have been swept away for this big day. The politics of who's in and who's out are silenced. The adults move fully into their adult skins, and the kids are everyone's main concern. Blue and orange balloons, white cakes, and white dresses—it's graduation day and the whole place is spruced up in the Amidon team colors of blue, orange, and white. The place feels bright and clean and hopeful. The big day is here: the fifth graders will walk across the stage and graduate.

I didn't realize this was such a big deal, but to these parents, many of whom did not graduate high school, graduating from elementary school is a significant achievement and they come out, dressed to the nines. The children look like angels, the girls in white and the boys in their suits and ties. The street urchins have received proper clothes as a result of donations from teachers and the community. Everyone looks sharp and the bad behaviors are set aside: the children know it's their time to shine.

Ms. Finch has her impressive chorus, "The Best in Southwest," tuned up to belt out some cheerful churchy songs and the cafeteria is packed. Folks are spilling out the back doors— grandmothers, mothers, aunties, and a few dads, many with their phone cameras on video, filming the big moment. The lucky ones will go out to a big lunch at Golden Corral and for a day they feel accepted, capable, celebrated. They are special; they have truly accomplished something in muscling through these elementary years. Ms. Finch's crew sways and sings, "This little light of mine, I'm gonna let it shine."

Sierra's Book

Sierra comes in at the end of the year and asks to see her composition book. She found reading and writing challenging, but loved the "feel" of pencil on paper and would fill the lines of her composition book with mostly incoherent sentences. Page after page, from front to back, she would write out her thoughts and stories. From margin to margin, she poured out her very best. The beauty of her effort shone through, despite the lapses in spelling and grammar. Sierra sits across from me and smiles, slowly paging reverently through the book. "Did a lotta work this year." She smiles at the pages. "A lotta work."

Music in the Halls (These Children Are Music) #3

Tunes emerge from the fabric of this place and seep into my brain, the blood of it, the vibrancy that is a part of every day at Amidon. I come to work and am immersed in it, a complete experience. There is nowhere to hide; everyone feels the energy of hope, the energy of hopelessness, the energy of love, the energy of abuse and neglect, all of it mixed in an incredible gumbo. A spicy brew that permeates the walls, the halls, the classrooms, the playground, the gym, a world that gets inside of me. This place changes a person forever, inside and out. This music will always be with me.

6

Under the Thumb of IMPACT and "High Stakes" Testing

The Specter of Michelle Rhee

Her dictatorial cloud hangs over this place. Her memory and presence, an ill wind. She showed little respect to this DC world—she blew it up, in fact. It's a blame game: how are the kids' testing scores so low and the teachers' ratings so high? Good question. Tough question. Her answer was to rip into the teachers. Her picture on the cover of *Time* with a broom was particularly galling. Word was, Rhee couldn't handle these kids for the few years she was a classroom teacher. She could not demonstrate proficiency. But none of that mattered—she came in and heads rolled.

IMPACT was Rhee's weapon, a scoring system that measures teachers and their classroom management and instruction. Rhee appeared and careers were ended, lives ruined, schools closed, and many Black folks were penciled out of their jobs. Some tough, smart, savvy teachers remained. Bring Rhee's name up in neighborhood schools and you'd hear shouts, catcalls. She held an infamous spot in the minds of DC teachers. She was the executioner. "Sure, change was needed, but not like that. They weren't all bad," Ms. Bluette tells me. "Some teachers had to go. Some were having the kids fold their laundry. Some would sleep all morning." Rhee implemented a teacher rating system, without adequately educating the teachers in its use, and used it to root out hundreds of teachers. Maybe some deserved it, but most of the teachers I met entered the profession because they wanted to teach; they wanted the kids to succeed, and they celebrated, dozens of times a day, the learning that was taking place amid the chaos and the layers of trauma, against all odds.

The IMPACT system is derived from corporate-style evaluations and data measurements; a system based on nine teaching practices. In addition, teachers are held responsible for the student's scores on standardized tests. Teacher's livelihoods now depended on the kids' test scores improving, not a little bit, but dramatically and suddenly. Without positive movement in test scores, a teacher would be gone. This was not what any teacher had signed up for and now many were stuck between trying to make this happen (without a set curriculum or understanding on how to magically accomplish this task) and losing everything—their jobs, their homes, even their families. It was a scourge. The biggest problem initially was that teachers were not formally and sufficiently trained in the pedagogy of IMPACT before they were observed, evaluated, and removed.

The school system, and my elementary school in particular, was in tatters, still reeling from this purge when I was hired. Staff were still adjusting to IMPACT, starting to resist and question some of the more heartless practices. I could see the chasm. One day you had a job, and a difficult one, and the next day strangers were in your room, taking notes, observing, observing, observing; the folks in suits and high heels kept coming in waves, "cleansing" the system. Teachers didn't know what hit them. We were left with the remains. The school was held together by duct tape and Band-Aids, a loose array of educational theories, financial incentives based on test scores, and classroom methodology.

"Massa" Educators

I arrive at Amidon in the middle of this fray and start to glean out major themes, discern what was driving this hope and confusion. I had read about Rhee in the media and had mixed feelings about her. The bullseye for the IMPACT system was situated squarely on the teachers' backs. Research shows that having high-quality teachers in the classroom can dramatically improve outcomes for high-poverty kids and help close the achievement gap. The idea is that if we get enough "rockstar" teachers, the inequities and inequalities in education will simply melt away. It's a fine concept, but there are numerous interwoven obstacles to the kids' learning besides hiring superperson teachers. A teacher cannot wave a magic wand and transform the entrenched problems caused by the complex consequences of poverty and family instability.

The disciples and inquisitors of this IMPACT gospel were the Master Educators. Ms. Barnett calls them "Massa Educators," and folks referred to working for DCPS as "being back on the plantation." These "instructional experts" descended on our rooms like storm clouds. It's a "gotcha" culture that accompanies their surprise visits. Teachers would religiously check the entry log for new visitors to see if "one of them" was in the building. Better to know and be one up on the draw instead of them catching you unawares. Sometimes, the administrative staff downstairs would give you a heads up. Other times, someone would oversee watching the parking lot to see if a strange car had pulled in. The code was "The British are coming," or "Any British here today?" You needed to be ready for a visit at any time. There was a covert, sneaky nature to these "visits." They are less about sustainable professional development and reaching educational "Big Goals," than they are about catching teachers off guard and undermining teacher confidence.

The master educators (or MEs) create a hyper culture of fear and paranoia. At any moment, someone might pop into a teacher's room and slay them with their pen until that teacher was out of a job. The teachers have little respect for these "experts," believing that they do not fully understand or care about the issues facing high-poverty schools; the teachers know that these outsiders couldn't survive ten minutes of actual teaching in their classrooms. To outlast the encounter and keep their jobs, most teachers put on a show. The whole process is often a charade, from the performance the teachers put on to the subjective and slap-dash evaluation that comes from the ME's forty-five-minute classroom visits. People who work in the school day after day knew what went on in people's classrooms; they knew who was doing a good job. To have a stranger briefly show up in a teacher's room, unannounced, with the power to have that teacher fired is a bizarre, insulting, unproductive, and often cruel practice.

Hide the "Trouble"

In any classroom, there were at least five or six difficult kids, either behaviorally, educationally, or both. When the "British" were around, a cat-and-mouse game commenced with teachers hiding these "trouble" kids in other teachers' rooms. Within the building, it was an accepted accommodation. Teachers could more easily teach an effective lesson (by ME standards) when they had kids who could read on grade level and sit still for a while. Smart teachers would have a Master Educator plan in place, and many kept a special lesson plan in a drawer just for these visits. They already knew which students they would need to extricate from their class.

When a ME arrived and asked for a certain teacher, a frantic shuffling of kids would often ensue. Panic would set in among the teachers because everyone knew the ME was on-site. Teachers would help each other as we knew it was highly unlikely any of us could keep our jobs with the wild kids in our classes. Working together, teachers planned the student deployments.

"When they come, will you take child X, Y and Z?"

"Okay. Then you'll take child A, B and C, right?"

Removing the worst behaved kids gave the teachers a chance to succeed. This kid swapping created comical juxtapositions and visual disjuncts, like Ms. Sampson dropping six first graders off in a fifth-grade classroom. The little ones sat on a rug in front of the big kids and colored, while Ms. Sampson, back in her room and freed from her "trouble" kids, gave her "highly effective" lesson.

Mishaps would occur. One time, Ms. Hall sent her "trouble" kids across the hall, telling Ms. Maxwell the British were here, while another ME was already in Ms. Maxwell's room conducting an evaluation. That did not end well for either of the teachers. The entire ME visit reeked of fear and absurdity, but the teachers did what they had to do to survive. If Central Office wanted this to look like a nice, tidy school with "regular" kids, then that is what the teachers would show them, at least for their forty-five-minute dog and pony show. It was a way of dealing with the true chaos, stress, disorder, dysfunction, and other maladies that enveloped the school. No one wanted to confront this truth: the teachers wanted their jobs, and most were dedicated to the kids. The shuffling of kids was the half-truth, the uneasy truce they drew with the outside world to keep their jobs. A compromise, a necessary deceit, driven by the need to survive in an impossible and unrealistic system.

Arc of the "Next" Superstar

"Just wait and see," Ms. Bluette said as we smiled at one another. We were discussing the sudden emergence of the administration's next "darling." Not that we were belittling another's success, but we knew how these things happened at Amidon. The administration was looking for a hero, the whole "Superperson" thing; someone to actually prove to them that what they were trying to do was the right thing, that it could be done. They sought the one person who would validate their assumptions about the hundred or more mostly well-meaning, dedicated, talented and trained teachers who had been chewed up and spat out from our school during the course of this untethered educational experiment.

So here she comes, Ms. Minton, with her fashionable clothes and her experience as a major in the army. She brings her military ideas to the classroom, and they work! The administration is ecstatic! Things go smoothly for a while, until the kids get tired of being barked at, of acting like little soldiers, of sitting through an incomprehensible lesson.

Ms. Minton is held up as a role model; the next star to

bail the administration out. It's confusing for the staff. Does the administration want us to adopt these practices? Do they want us to lock it down and yell at the kids? Most of our professional development sessions are about understanding the whole child, meeting the child where they are at. Do they want us to run our rooms like a military school? What are we doing schoolwide?

The fraying begins. Before you know it, the underlying emotional issues and learning deficits of the kids in her room come to the surface. These are children, not young adults to be molded into soldiers. This is education, not all-out conformity. The lockdown, top-down model will only take you so far. A seething frustration is stirring beneath the surface and youngsters are poised to explode.

Less than two years later, Ms. Minton was taking extended periods of time off for chest pains, heart trouble, and fatigue. She threw everything into helping the kids the best way she knew how and was now paying the price.

"Teach it Yourself"

"Here," you want to tell them. "You take the marker. Here! You teach these kids." There is an inherent absurdity to the steady stream of coaches and observers who come into our rooms. They come with their laptops and educational theories, but they don't have to live day in and day out with the human tragedy and toxic mix of poverty and below-grade readers thrust into this swirl of unrealistic expectations—unrealistic as to how far some of the kids can go; unrealistic as to how fast the kids can move; unrealistic as to the methods to help the kids; unrealistic as to the kids' very deep and close-to-the-surface psychological problems and behavioral difficulties. They step with authority into my classroom to observe. Teachers, who see and live inside the human tragedy at Amidon, want to yell at these observers: "See that kid there? Please! Please! Please! Pick up a book and sit and read with that child before he tears my room to pieces." But instead, the stern-faced observers type away, ignoring the chaos, an inhumane witness to yet another child going to pieces. They *observe* a child's meltdown; they *observe* the teacher's anxiety; they *record* it all for the teacher's later conference; and then they snap up their laptop and leave, that teacher's career in their hands, without a smile, a nod, or a goodbye.

Disservice

The general education teacher's lament is, "These kids aren't getting their hours; where's the special education (SPED) teacher?" A common refrain in the building, meaning that the SPED kids, who have a prescribed number of hours they should be receiving in small-group specialized instruction, are not being serviced. The general education teachers need relief from the intense pressure and emotional demands that stem from these children's trauma, insecurities, and disabilities. The SPED kids need the extra attention of smaller groups and the regular teacher does not have the bandwidth to provide this for them. Time is never the teacher's friend; teachers know, as the minutes tick by, things will begin to unravel. The SPED kids will hold it together for a while but eventually the educational and behavioral challenges that landed them in SPED surface and they explode.

The chaos and lack of adequate resources within the building necessitates that SPED teachers become ad hoc troubleshooters; they are pulled in a dozen different directions. The SPED teachers are called to do testing; the SPED students aren't being served. The SPED teachers are called to be a substitute because the school can't get substitutes; the SPED students aren't being served. A troubled kid needs a walk to calm down; the other SPED students are not getting their hours. The SPED teachers have a long IEP meeting; the SPED students aren't being served. The SPED teacher has to have a hearing at Central Office about not serving the SPED students; ironically, the SPED students aren't being served.

With a school in such a state of stress and disorder, this deficiency in providing services for the SPED students causes multiple problems that have a ripple effect. Generally, SPED students are far below grade level in reading and math and usually exhibit the most problem behaviors. The very reason many have been assigned SPED hours for interventions is they don't function well in a large group setting. So, the problem compounds itself. Teachers are already overwhelmed with the large numbers of SPED students in the class, sometimes this can be 50 percent or more of the total class enrollment of thirty or more students. This puts an untenable burden on the classroom teacher. They are expected to plan each lesson for six different grade levels of ability, as SPED kids can range from one to five years below grade level. Then they have to try and adapt the classroom to myriad behavior problems that range from oppositional-defiant, ADHD, autism, learning disabilities, cognitive issues and more. Most of these SPED kids have already adapted ingenious ways of avoiding work and disrupting the class. Rightfully so, these children are embarrassed, and anxiety ridden about what their peers think of them. The whole system that is put in place to help SPED kids fails when a school suffers such an imbalance between ideal culture and real student concerns. The scales tip: disorder becomes the rule of the day. Most teachers become incredibly adept at handling these problems, but it puts an enormous strain on school morale. It cheats too many students out of a quality education and causes many teachers to fail or leave. This discordant problem will not go away until adequate resources are set aside to properly serve the SPED population.

Revolving Door

In the beginning, I learned everyone's name. I felt like we were a team, pulling for the same cause: to teach these students. Over time, it became more and more about the adults, more and more about the paycheck, then finally about survival. In the beginning, we had common goals. I felt part of a mission. By my fifth year, when new teachers came on board, I rarely learned their names. The few of us who remained size up the new ones.

"He'll never last, or she'll never make it." Onward they come into this great maw of DCPS, before they are chewed up and spat out. No training can prepare a teacher for this combat zone. An educator here needs to be of a certain ilk— they need to be able to take a punch, to be able to get up off the mat after being knocked down; they need to be persistent, to have resolve, and, truly, to be more than a little bit crazy to survive. Ms. Bluette told me one day, "You know how I knew you were going to make it? Because you listen, you adapt, and you're crazy. I see it in your eyes sometimes and believe me, I've seen crazy." More than one hundred different teachers walked in and then out of our elementary school doors during my five years and only four of us had lasted. Figure that one out. What does that have to say about DCPS?

So many teachers came and went, I would just nod to the new faces. We would end up using teachers without licenses, while certified, capable people were scattered to the wind. Children, knowing little structure at home, came to a building without constancy. This is not a recipe for sustainability and growth. This is, instead, a climate of instability, and insecurity, characterized by fear from top to bottom; a fear propagated daily by a deluded Central Office that imagines a world of education considerably different from the one teachers experience. Every year, DCPS drags a community to the finish line. Every year is defined by unmet expectations, where the kids fall further and further behind.

How can a dedicated teacher contribute to, and help build, a school culture when DCPS is constantly throwing new plans at new teachers, with people running around senselessly, with no institutional memory and no fertile ground? All the activity swirls away in the chaos of kids misunderstood, not being served, and not learning. This vicious cycle is repeated year after year, marked by unrealistic expectations and increasingly ignorant policies. One earnest and well-meaning teacher at a time is flushed through the system and out the other side.

Dirty Little Secret

Nobody hears about this on the news, when the media is ripping apart public schools again and singing the praises of charter schools and school choice. Unwanted charter school kids arrive at Amidon after the official attendances have been completed for the schools. They come after the amount of money paid to the school for each child served has been determined. Early October—that's when the charter schools start to unload. My first year, Ms. Bluette told me, "Watch out for that crew. Those are the real tough nuts. The ones the charter schools threw out."

The charter schools tolerate the special education kids, the ones that need extra help, just long enough to get funding, then they "paper" them out; they keep a list of misbehaviors, documenting the problems until they have the opportunity to ship those kids out. Out of their back pockets come the kids' list of transgressions and—*boom!*—the child is tossed out of the charter school and shipped to their home public school. Students arrive intermittently throughout October and perhaps behave well for a week or two. When the honeymoon's over, that's when the real problems begin to emerge, the true trauma, the significant learning disabilities. These kids will hang on the doors, brawl, "buck up" on the teachers, spit on kids, break down and cry for hours. Everyone on the front lines knows we need to figure out what to do with the kids with significantly entrenched behavioral challenges. The public schools have no choice. The charter schools can throw kids out after they receive their check. This is not a level playing field. This is what happens when test results take priority over children, when a false ideology is twisted into a truth.

Ms. Sampson Knows Her IMPACT

Ms. Sampson moved with a confidence and grace that was rare at our school. She had seen the other teachers come and go and was determined to remain. Teaching was her calling, her profession. She was a true professional; she could manage a class, understood how to scaffold instruction for the lower kids, and she knew how to guide her instruction to help the kids master standardized tests. IMPACT had left an enormous impression on her. She had seen her friends confused by IMPACT and left without jobs. She studied IMPACT, asked questions, and was generally proactive about how it might affect her; she was not going to let strangers come into her room and tell her what she should do. The MEs would give her their observation results, and enraged, she would start making notes all over the observation with her red pen, telling the observer in no uncertain terms what they had missed.

Ms. Sampson was a wise woman who helped me understand the ways of IMPACT sufficiently to eventually be rated highly effective. "IMPACT!" she would say, already irate. "Whoa, hold on now, let me tell you a thing or three about IMPACT. No stranger is going to take Ms. Sampson's job." And off she'd rant—about "these people" telling her what to do and how to run her classroom, strangers trying to force her out, interlopers who had no idea what it was like teaching in a high-poverty school but who had the gall to tell her how she could improve her lesson. This was not going to fly with Ms. Sampson, she was a fighter through and through and a true warrior-teacher. She was one of the four of us who survived all five years I was there.

The Testing Game

The kids know that testing is a game. The whole thing is hyped up. There are test pep rallies and visits from supervisors and administrators, all bowing to the sacredness of standardized tests. What do the children think? How do they feel? How about the ones who know they won't do well? What are we telling them? That they will fail at what is being presented as the most important part of their education? Where did the focus on the "whole child" go? The contradictions are too broad to bridge.

Testing, Prodding, and Torturing the Special Education Kids

A particularly malevolent aspect of this ever-present testing environment was the frequent prodding of the kids who were below grade level. They were constantly told, and shown, how they were not passing muster, labeled below basic, given assessments that harrowed them dozens of times a year. This persistent form of indifference was managed by teachers in different ways. Some would give the kids treats, some would give them extra recess. Something had to be done so that you would not feel like a malevolent person subjecting young children to more and more dispiriting tests.

It was painful, trying to get the special education kids to comply with doing something they knew they could not do. The kids would react in all manner of ways—tearing up the tests, running out of the school, hitting each other. They devised clever ways of avoiding the stress and torture of knowing they had failed again at something they did not understand. Their inner-knowing wedged between the idea of school as a place to learn and grow versus yet another place to be humiliated. School became their torment, and effort became an insistent sign of their failure. Subjected to this, dragged screaming through test after test, the kids' inner intelligence told them to RUN or ACT OUT or REBEL. Then we suspended them or scolded them or coerced them or chastised them for doing what any reasonable human would do in response to such cruelty.

Heard from the Halls (Testing Week)

"I can't do this! You never taught us this! I can't do this white man shit."

"Look, just fill in the bubbles nice and clean. Do the best you can."

"Please don't rip the test up. We need this test!"

"If you fill in all the bubbles, I'll give you a cookie."

"Last year, you all were chasing me around the building and

out to the street just so I wouldn't tear up your nasty test."

"How do you spell, *I don't know?*"

Montoyo's Big Day

This was the big day, the day the test scores were released. Teacher's jobs and reputations hung in the balance. I pulled up the data on the computer and was astounded; Montoyo, a special education student, had scored 44 percent in reading, the top percentage in all of fourth grade. I had to check it again to be sure. It was true. This young boy read at first-grade level at best, and here he was leading the class. How did this happen?

Well, the test was multiple choice. It was administered by another teacher other than his classroom teacher, with fidelity. That teacher had no reason to cheat, she was being observed while giving the test. Aware of Montoyo's reading level, teachers suspected that Montoyo just happened to color in the right bubbles. Although 44 percent in many other schools would be an abject failure, at Amidon it was top of the class.

Montoyo had blown it up. The analysis of data and breaking down the components of education into slices of the Common Core had been thrown to the wind. We were stunned. As special education coordinator, I had to assure the other teachers that I did not give the test. The whole process now had a measure of absurdity. If, after all the talking and planning and studying and analysis, Montoyo could get the top score in the class, what did that say about the process as a whole?

When I told Montoyo of his amazing feat, he nodded his head. "Naww." Then his big eyes brightened, and he smiled and said, "Really? Really?"

Expert Lesson

Once, a former master educator came in to demonstrate a model lesson as part of a job interview. The principal, two instructional coaches, and three other adults were in the room with twenty-five kids. As the ME started her lesson, a girl stood up and smacked another girl right across the face. The educator either didn't notice or chose not to notice and continued her out-of-the-box lesson that hit the high marks and checked off the top instructional techniques. Meanwhile, two more fights broke out, two kids doodled away, another drew pictures, another threw paper at friends, one kid left the room crying, and another got up and wandered around the room, whistling. The educator soldiered through. At the end, school leaders thought she had done a great job and wanted to hire her. The collective torpor mirrored DCPS's warped lens. The modeling of a "perfect lesson" is more important than true student engagement.

Suspensions

"We need to get T'wan out! He needs a few days off. You need a break, T'wan?" As the school becomes increasingly out of control, teachers look for a reprieve, and suspending a child is an easy way out. The threats come in waves to the really troubled kids. Hey, it's a reasonable thought. Some of these kids will tear your room up and then, after order is restored, tear it up again the same day. Significant challenges keep the teachers from maintaining order and delivering quality instruction. Exacerbating the situation, the kids go home every night to the same environment that led them to adopt their destructive and often violent behaviors in the first place. The kids get tossed out of school for two, three days, some even a whole week or more, and then what? Sure, the tension in the school goes down and the teachers can take a deep breath, no longer subjected to unrelenting aggression, but what about that child? That child is, once again, marginalized, ostracized. They won't or can't do the work packet that's sent home, and thus they fall further and further behind. They sit around all day watching junk on TV, playing video games, or are out running the streets. Some suspended kids wander the perimeter of the school, peeking in at what they're missing. Maybe they didn't get fed at home, and they're missing their free school meals. When they return to school, they fall back in with the same crew and the cycle begins anew.

The Real Deal

Ms. DeVann had come here from Central Office, where plans were made and records kept. Her mission was to clean up "school culture." With her British accent and curt demeanor, the staff dubbed her "Nanny 9-1-1" as in "There's a fight in the cafeteria, better call Nanny 9-1-1." She had a true challenge on her hands, straightening up this place. One of her jobs was to help me with the afterschool athletic program. As the kids converged on the back field, wrestling, fighting, cursing, and crying, running back into the school to run the halls, running off the school grounds and into the street, she looked at me and said, "Mr. J., I had no idea. Central Office has no idea what this is really like. They sit around all day, looking at data. They don't know it's like this down here!"

Quick Fix

Out here in suburbia, at a dinner party or gathering, people are always interested in telling me their solutions for high-poverty DC schools. There is a pervasive perception that the world down there is a hopeless situation. Some shake their heads, and say, "What's the use?" Blind as I was to their own privileges, they don't know the hopeful faces of the kids I teach every day. They don't want to know how many teachers and parents do care deeply about addressing inequity, courageously showing up each day to help children learn and grow.

Still others are rampant supporters of charter schools, as if these schools will somehow radically alter the lives of children from high-poverty areas. Charter schools in DC have had mixed results at best. Despite not having to educate many of the toughest special education and behaviorally challenged kids, they still struggle to outperform DCPS.

I recall reading about David Simon, writer of *The Wire*, discussing poverty in a speech. [4] He said that we have decided as a society to tolerate a certain percentage of poverty, inequity, and

4 Lanre Bakare, "David Simon: 'There are now two Americas. My country is a horror show'." *The Guardian*, December 7, 2013

despair. We have resolved as a community that if poor people are geographically confined and don't infiltrate mainstream culture, we can ignore the problems that they endure.

I understand people wondering why the achievement gap hasn't been "fixed." I had no idea of the immense challenges and stresses that poverty places on children and their education. I think of Martin Luther King, Jr. and wonder what he would say. He knew that a country was only as strong as its weakest member. Until we stop throwing quick fixes at these problems, they will never go away. Quick fixes cause schools to pretend that things are working, to pretend that everything is all right, when the school is falling apart from within. Only through long-term commitments, including wrap-around health and social services, will we ever have a reprieve from this desolation.

Outliers, All

When everyone is not together, when one of us is lost, then all are lost. When we are not teaching the lowest kids, when we decide to just teach the eager ones that want to learn, we have made an unjust bargain. We are writing children off before they have even started and if we give up hope on them, who do they have?

The children are looking to the teachers, the teachers to the administration, the administration to Central Office, Central Office to the chancellor. People want a path to succeed; everyone wants to know what to do and how to serve the kids. The children want to feel safe, nurtured, understood, and challenged. This is attempted through a haze of misunderstandings, a haze of unrealistic expectations, a haze of not seeing the kids for who they really are, a haze of not seeing teachers as adults, a haze of not grasping the neighborhood and situations these children come from. The end result is all of us become outliers grasping for a lifeline.

7

THE PERVADING VIOLENCE

Violence in the Air

A violence permeates the air—the students toward the teachers, the teachers toward the students, the administrators toward the teachers, the superintendent toward the administrators; it is a vicious thread that sets the tone for the whole school. Compassion comes in small doses. The whole staff is in hyper mode to help the kids, to keep their job, to stay out of trouble, and to stay on point, hoping not to be observed when the class is falling apart. Violence informs the language of emails, the language of dissent, the language of instruction. There is nowhere to hide.

You Need to Be Tough

Ms. Hall, a longtime DC teacher, counseled me. "These kids don't respect kindness; you have to dig down, dig deep. Be tougher than you ever imagined, tougher than you've ever been. They say talk to these kids like you would your own kids, but your own kids don't act like this."

She grabbed my arm and drew me closer. "They don't respect you unless you are tough. These kids don't respect white people, all that 'Please, sweetie, this and, sweetie, that' stuff—they think you're funny; they think you're soft. When you talk to these kids politely, they know they can run you over, that you can't get up in their face, that you won't smack them around like their mommas."

"Sometimes you have to make that phone call," she continued, "and when the woman on the other end says, 'Oh, I'm gonna fix that, don't you worry, I'll get him good,' know for sure why you made that call."

Janissa is Gone

I get to school and hear the news and immediately imagine the worst. My chest tightens and my pulse grows fast. There's an inevitability to tragedy that comes with some of these children's lives. I think of the sickening horrors that ten-year-old Janissa, my student, has endured and imagine the worst. She's out working the streets, or captured by the wrong crew, spinning off into risky behaviors and danger.

When you've been exploited so viciously, so terribly, what options do you even imagine? I can't finish reading some of the kids' case histories. Janissa's was one of the worst. She's a cute child, too, which only adds to the nightmare that arises when I envision her reality. Not knowing any better, once she batted her eyes and said, "We can have a fun time if you want, Mr. J. I like you." I held a conference with her adopted mom about it, and still Janissa thought it was funny.

I know her, Janissa, as a bright little girl in my class reading a folktale, "The Coyote and the Star," holding her fractured dreams together, wanting to be a child. And here she was, ten going on eighteen and a runaway, out all night, no one knows where she is. The streets suck kids up in a sickening wind. Is it inevitable? How can you stop this evil wind? I try to see the kids with fresh eyes or maybe I'm afraid; I can't let in all that pain—little girls raped before their teens and traded off to strangers for drugs.

Ms. Taylor, the social worker, told me the cold score, which ones might end up on the street hustling, and now it's on the news. Janissa has run away, she was last seen with two male teenagers. Horrors you don't want to imagine are all too real for this child. I keep checking my phone for the news, the sad news of a lost, lost child.

Make the Right Choice?

The final bell has rung and the kids spill onto the playground to wait for dismissal. Summer is in the air, the school year is winding down, and old beefs are boiling over. Fights pop up like wildfires and before you know it two ten-year-old kids are wailing on each other. Real punches being thrown, both kids hitting harder with each blow. The humane thing to do is to break it up and, as with dozens of fights before, I step in and grab a kid's arm and pull him to safety. He was still "bucking up" and swinging, his shirt was drenched in sweat, tears gushing down his face. I held him back from the fray until, finally, the other kid's mom came to pick him up and tempers cooled. Later Ms. Bluette warned me. "You need to watch that. Someone catches you on their phone and you'll be on the six o'clock news."

Amidon on the Nightly News (Again)

"Did you see that white man? You know, the head of the PTA, that lawyer who's trying to fix the school? Mister Whitey Whatshisname."

"Those boys was fightin' in the cafeteria and he dragged that boy right outta there. Grabbed him by the arm and dragged him across the floor! It's on the cameras."

"See the reporter out there across the street?"

"Gonna be on the Channel 7 news!"

A Moment of Fame

The violence of the kids' lives spills over into school. The violence of our society, the want for notoriety, what passes for celebrity spreads like a virus into the classrooms. The kids can be devious and will manipulate matters to get what they want. And now with cell phones, they plan meet-ups, fights, they'll group-jump a kid and then post the video online.

Here it was. Raven and Tiara snuck down to the empty gym. This was it, girl on girl, a total smackdown. They knew when the gym would be empty. They had two friends there to video the fight, to record this vicious battle where, screaming, they kicked each other, tore at each other's hair, tugged on braids, ripped clothes, punched each other's heads again and again. The fight's out there now on YouTube, spread across the DMV and beyond. Amidon in the news—the bad news—again.

The Violence Within

Word spread quickly. Ms. Hall had called Diamond's mom one too many times and now she was coming up. We heard that Diamond's mom took her out in the hall and when Diamond sassed her, her mom smacked her right in the mouth. Here it was now, right in school. Lines were being crossed. By what now? What trust did we have with the kids when school was no longer a safe haven for them? How could we put ourselves on a pedestal as educators when we participated in this violence by calling the parents in and then turning a blind eye?

The Story of DeAndre

I knew when I met DeAndre that he was trouble. DeAndre had a wild eye, an eye for danger that even made me afraid. He might do anything at any time and loved being in the middle of any fray. I pulled him out of class after he had bullied each kid into giving him their pencil: "Give me your pencil, give me your pencil," and so on down the line.

We sat in the stairwell, and he told me about his dad being in jail. DeAndre was already notorious, had been on house arrest, wearing an ankle monitor at ten for robbing someone on the street. "Do you really want to go to jail? You gotta turn this around, son."

For a moment, lucidity cut through the wildness of his mind. He took a deep breath and sighed, "No, no. But how can you change?"

Summer Ice Cream

The tales come to you, what the kids were up to over the summer. Every kid loves a nice cool ice cream on a hot summer
day. So, it was on one of those sticky, relentless, swampy DC
summer late afternoons, that DeAndre and his twin brother
DeLandre walked into the Safeway. They had been staring at
that freezer full of ice cream all summer long. They'd walk past
it, not being able to buy anything, just to look at the different
popsicles and special treats. One day, this game of Tantalus
had gone on long enough. Middle of the day, they walked right
into the freezer and started feasting on the ice cream, ice cream
sandwiches, ice pops, and chocolate cones. It took a while until
people noticed them, tearing off wrappers and satisfying their
long-carried cravings. Popsicle sticks on the ground, surrounded by wrappers, they continued their feast. They wouldn't let
the store manager in the freezer and took turns, holding the
door locked.

Finally, the police were called. The boys reveled in their abun-
dance and grinned their wild boy grins at all the attention. The
police laughed it off at first and then got flat-out frustrated at
the boys' stubbornness and refusal to comply. When the game
had finally ended and the boys had had their fill, they proudly
emerged with their white T-shirts stained with the colors of the
ice cream rainbow, rubbing their bellies, and laughing, until the
cops led them to the nearby police station. A few people out
on the street applauded the boys and another tale in DeAndre
and DeLandre's defiant legacy was cemented in the oral history
of the hood.

When DeAndre Shot up the Zoo

Stories trickle back to you from the hood: who has been shot,
who was stealing cars, who was dealing drugs. DeAndre's notoriety followed him after he left Amidon. I heard on the news
that a juvenile had been arrested for shooting into a crowd at

the National Zoo. Word carried through the neighborhood pipeline that it was my former student, DeAndre. I wonder what I could have done differently. Was this inevitable?

Name in the News. Name on a T-Shirt

"We want you kids in the news for good things, helpful things, not for being a name on a T-shirt."

Not dead, is what she meant. Not acting the fool and ending up dead, is what Ms. Bluette meant.

Weapons of Survival

Tyrone had been caught bringing in two knives last week. As a safety precaution, I oversaw checking his backpack. Every morning, I would take him into the conference room, and he would empty out his bag. I would make sure he was not sneaking anything dangerous into the building. Everything looked okay, and I was starting to think this kind of oversight was a waste of time, that the knives were a one-time affair, but as I reached into the back of his pack, I found a screwdriver.

"What's this?"

"Screwdriver, whatcha think?"

"What do you plan on doing with this?"

"My cousin said if they mess with me, shut them up with this. It's for protection."

"You know I have to take it."

"No way, give it back! Give it back! They're going to jump me!"

Tyrone exploded, tears streaming down his face. He came at me, and I avoided him as best I could until security came and contained him. Then he broke free and ran around the room and knocked three framed paintings off the wall and shards of glass scattered everywhere. Immediately, he picked up a big shard of glass and said, "I'm gonna cut myself! I'm gonna do it!" Ms. Wingate, the social services rep, had arrived. Tyrone was focused on me and she entered the room behind him. In one of the bravest acts I have witnessed, she came up behind Tyrone and snatched the glass from his hand.

All in a Day's Work

Calling attendance, one by one, then—"T'asia? T'asia? Anyone know where T'asia is?"

"She was shot."

"What?"

"Yeah, shot last night on the street. Playing in front of her house."

"No, is she okay?"

"Don't know. They took her away in an ambulance."

So, you move directly from not knowing if one of your students is dead to teaching the required English block. You're expected to switch on a dime from the uncertainty of your student's death to focus on the other twenty-five students and their needs.

I'll have to wait for lunch to call home and find out if T'asia's dead, crippled, suffering . . .

The Rawness and Hope of Youth

These children are so honest, so direct in their indirection, so readable in their deceit and sorrow. They are trying to make it and, switching up on you or not, there always seems to be a big smile in there somewhere, a joy at the indisputable bounciness of youth. No matter how crushed or put-on or put down, they run and laugh and smile. Youth can't help itself, youngness shines through; everything has a purity for a time, a greenness, a wonder, a hopefulness that still exists. You can't lie to these kids. Try and they suck their teeth and say, "Oh, all right, got you," meaning they got you dead, they know what you're about, you're just another person trying to pull the wool over their eyes.

When they meet you, when they greet you, their whole world is there right in front of you, their brown eyes reading you, straight up. It's all on the table. They may be way low down, they may be hiding something, they may be an inch away from a meltdown, you can feel all of it, these precious gifts of life force, "these babies" opened for the world to see and what do they see? Something that is wrong, a world that wants to take from them, that wants to hurt them. Beautiful babies singing into the world, many soon to be crushed by the odds, by the hatred, by the drugs, by the hopelessness. A mentor visiting from the FBI tells it true. "It's sad, but you know, less than 2 percent of these kids will ever go to college, let alone graduate." Where do they go from here?

8

THIS IS THE END

Spiral

The teachers came to a breaking point. So many seminars, speeches, and pep talks made to good people ready to run up any hill under any circumstance and yet without an overall coherent mission, it all fell apart. The stresses of the school tore away the knowledge of adulthood and everyone was dealing with their inner child, the damaged one, the one that still hurts and needs to be healed. The school environment became raw, professional values were tossed to the wind, and adults yelled at each other, yelled at the administration, screamed at the kids. Desperately seeking some sense of control, the volume was raised, the tenor of the building escalated, everything became amplified, and everybody suffered. Everyone was searching for some semblance of order, some island in their storm, some way of addressing the world, only to be thrown back to the all-too-familiar world of chaos and distrust where possibility is truly lost.

Grit and persistence can only last for so long. The desire to help kids can only be sustained over time if there is a clear plan, a plan that can be achieved, where the teachers and the students feel some degree of success. Otherwise, you spiral downward, which we did . . .

One Percent Proficient?

The PARCC test scores had come in and they weren't good: 1 percent proficient in English and 2 percent in Math. DCPS had switched from the easier DC-CAS test, but still, that low? How could we ever get to 50 or 60 percent? Veils had been ripped off. Truth was thundering down. Heads were going to roll. Was this really where the kids and the school were? What now?

Pirate Ship

The place had become a pirate ship, everyone out for themselves, no one trusting anyone, teachers poised to stab each other in the back. There was no job security, not with these kids, not with this leadership, these expectations. Everyone had their own take on things, everyone going in their own direction to survive, to survive and then what? This line of thought went no further. The stakes were raised even higher. More unannounced observers started walking through the rooms. Not even a note afterward. They type and type and observe and observe and you had no idea where it's going. Central Office? To the superintendent? To the principal? You're stuck in this bizarre test tube with the kids, tensions rising, fights breaking out, rumors spreading like malignant vapors, everyone on edge, with no safe harbor.

How did we turn teaching kids into a cut-throat enterprise? Every person for themselves, with no moral ground, the atmosphere rife with innuendo and rumors? No one felt good about their job. Everyone was on edge and looking over their shoulders. No one trusted anyone else. The adults in the building were despondent over their failures, tortured over their failure to obtain the desired results.

Were the expected outcomes reasonable? Were they justified? Achievable? Will I lose my job? Is all this worth it? What mission am I accomplishing? What directives am I following? More questions than answers. All of which was invariably followed by sleepless nights, self-medicating, denial, and avoidance. On and on. More parades of people coming through the classrooms with their laptops and notepads, prying, prodding, checking, suggesting, critiquing, and the teachers trying to keep a lid on it all. They tried to keep these children in line, keep them learning, somehow tap into higher-level thinking: fostering a "growth mindset." Teachers strived to keep some modicum of control, living under the constant dread that at any time his or her room could be invaded by strangers who don't introduce themselves. You're not supposed to say "hi" or ask them who they are. "Just keep teaching," they tell you. It's inhuman. They held your job at the tip of their typing fingers. Or did they? All was uncertain.

Two Trains Running

Teachers were losing their grip on the fourth- and fifth-grade hall. After spring break, beefs, grudges, and tensions were running high. The kids can only hold it together for so long. When the special education (SPED) kids aren't receiving their required services, it puts an enormous strain on the teachers. Eighteen out of thirty-six fourth grade students were SPED. The SPED teachers were being pulled in a dozen different directions. The general education teachers kept saying it, "These kids are not being served," but the priorities of the SPED kids fell to the bottom of the list.

There were two trains running. The school was becoming less adept at handling the behaviors of the kids just as the pressure from Central Office for sudden change was mounting. Then, a huge brawl broke out in the hall between the fourth- and fifth-grade classrooms. The kids, coming back from lunch and recess, were already riled up. They were shouting, yelling, screaming, crying, and full-out fighting. The superintendent, Dr. Robinson, walked into this scenario and watched. She wanted to see how the school would handle the crisis. Problem was, the principal, Ms. Hilton, was nowhere to be found. She was paged and never showed up. The teachers were put in the impossible position of breaking up a brawl and the superintendent stood back and then reported that the teachers just watched the kids tear each other apart.

Rumors had been going around for months about the principal disappearing from school for periods of time. The brawl marked the moment when the school turned south with finality. The stress, the lack of leadership and resources necessary to run a decent school, the toxicity of the staff, the relentless pressure from Central Office, and the constant, intense, and often perplexing behaviors of the kids who needed us finally brought about this grand implosion.

She's Gotta Go

Things were out of control. The quiet teachers hunkered down in their rooms. Some were whispering, others yelling about "you know who." "She's gotta go! She has got to go!" was a constant refrain. Resentment grew, no one felt safe. The school was in an uproar with the drama circling around the principal. Ms. Hilton had come in five years earlier on high hopes with a new, shining staff, me included, ready to tackle the achievement gap. She was fully committed and worked ridiculously long hours to try and turn the school around. Now she's lying? Some said they saw her out in the parking lot with a strange guy. She left school without telling anyone. She was not where she said she was when the big fight went down. She was not downstairs helping out in the kindergarten classrooms. Could this be true?

Ms. Sampson's Moment of Truth

Dr. Robinson had decided that she was going to let Ms. Hilton go but wanted the teachers to stay. They had totally cleaned house five years ago and the community did not want to endure that much disruption again. The idea was to have a meeting to get to the bottom of the underlying problems at the school. Noble idea, but Dr. Robinson had no idea of the deep festering divisions and problems.

The stage was set, and teachers and staff were sitting in a big circle in the library. Friends and foes, more than fifty people staring and glaring at each other. Folks had been waiting a long time for this, for a time to vent, for a time to spill dirt, for a time to tell the superintendent what had *really* been going on in the school. Things had never been out on the table. People were afraid that if they told the truth, they might lose their job. The usual way of handling these problems was to bitch about it with a few friends. This only caused divisions to become wider and resentments to grow deeper.

Ms. Sampson had been biting her lip for too long. She'd been endeavoring to look the other way, to hold it all inside. Now, she finally had her chance to clean the slate. Get everything out into the open. She had been teaching at Amidon Elementary for years before the big changes of IMPACT began, and she saw many of her hard-working friends and colleagues thrown to the curb by the Rhee revolution. Ms. Sampson was not impressed with how IMPACT was being wielded as a weapon against good teachers. She was not impressed with the lack of commitment and acumen of the new people who had come in to turn the school around.

Finally, she had her audience, and like a volcano with hot lava roiling just beneath the surface, Ms. Sampson was ready to blow. She waited for her moment, until others had told their stories, and then she commanded center stage. "Okay, now. Okay, it's time for Ms. Sampson to have her say and this has been a long time coming, believe you me." She launched into a firehose spray of complaints against the administration, the teachers who slacked off or who "don't know how to teach," against anyone, who, in her eyes, had not put the children front and center. Dr. Robinson listened stunned, without moving.

No one was without some fault here, and people slouched back in their chairs hoping not to be singled out in Ms. Sampson's torrent of accusations. "Oh yes," she went on, "Ms. Sampson's going to tell what she has seen and put up with in this place. This is supposed to be a school, people! A place of learning, a school! What I want to know is why the principal is sneaking off across the street to have Starbucks with her friends and then having little chit-chats about this person and that person? Oh! I know what they're saying. I know about all the little cliques in here and what people do and say to get promoted. What are we teaching these kids, anyway? I mean, c'mon people!" On she went for a good fifteen minutes. Most teachers were startled, some terrified, some amused. Everyone knew that this was not the new beginning Dr. Robinson had envisioned.

Final Bell

I sat on the outside steps, as I did most days in the spring. It was such a pleasant spot, with the dappled afternoon light filtering through the old oak trees. I felt planted, rooted, as the kids ran off and disappeared into the busyness of the city. Cries of "See ya, Mr. J.," and "Mr. J! Mr. J!" rang out as I gazed into their departing eyes and waved to the students who had captivated me through the long school days. I had double-checked my room, under the desks and chairs and in the closets, to make sure no child was hiding from the summer to come.

Bernard, my mini-me, shuffled out with two of his friends. He stopped in front of me, put his hand on my shoulder, patted me. "So, Mr. J, see you next year? You coming back?" knowing the unpredictable shuffling of teachers and adults that was a constant in his world. I hadn't sorted it all out yet. I hadn't really had the time to think on it. His question, his needs, silenced me. Bernard laughed nervously. "You are coming back, right?"

9

Moving On

Have Seen Both Sides

It all blew up. Between the finger pointing, the accusations, the students' meager gains, the rumors about the principal's absences, and confusion surrounding my IMPACT score, it came time for me to leave. The principal and assistant principal were let go, the official end of our five-year journey. I didn't have the will to take on yet another valiant attempt at transforming the ravages of multigenerational poverty here at Amidon. No more miracles were expected to appear on the horizon. I couldn't pretend that my understanding of the trials that lay ahead and the resources and expectations that were needed to alleviate those challenges were going to significantly differ from the past.

In my five years at Amidon, I experienced the gamut of teaching opportunities and challenges. I had been rated highly effective and was truly highly effective. I had also been rated effective and even minimally effective for one semester. I was the same person and the same teacher throughout those shifting experiences. The major difference between those dynamics was the constancy and quality of services that the special education children received. In my most effective years, the special education kids were nurtured and taught in small groups that maximized their learning potential. They were able to meet their goals, which reflected the grade level at which they were operating. In the other years, the kids were not getting their service hours and I was left to teach a class that ranged across years of educational skill level; while partially possible, through arduous effort and planning, this was not a formula for long-term success.

There was no new savior, no new principal who would be able to transform the school. It would take a lot more than that. Most people I worked with had given their all—striving to help the kids and work with the system. After I resigned, my final correspondences from DCPS were some friendly texts from fellow teachers and missives from Central Office about an appeal I'd made on my IMPACT score for that year. A data entry error lowered my official score from the one I had earned and deserved.

Central Office was doing its best to imitate the Office of Circumlocution from Dickens's *Little Dorrit*. I received three separate communications from DCPS sent by certified mail. The first letter informed me the IMPACT team approved my appeal. The second letter said the chancellor's office did not approve my appeal. The third time, the chancellor's office advised me to disregard their previous note, my appeal had been approved. So, there it was, Central Office, to the very end, not realizing that their incompetence and confusion demoralizes real human beings on the other end of their evaluation system. All along, I also was receiving emails from various DCPS entities telling me that as a highly effective teacher they wanted my input on new directions; emails stating they wanted me to know how important and valuable I was to the system and how appreciative they were.

The same inconstancy that haunts the children and their world, haunts the teachers. No one is on firm ground. It was painful to leave the kids behind, painful to leave the close friendships that were forged under these extraordinary conditions, painful to not help the kids more. Central Office wants you; they don't want you; you're doing great; you're doing lousy. How can they expect teachers to sort it all out without going crazy? It was time to move on. It no longer made sense to tie my passion, talent, and ambition to DCPS. Just like the anonymous children who vanish into the city streets, I joined the legions of DCPS teachers who disappear into other jobs, other professions, other lives.

Learning to Find a Way

In these pages, I have shared reflections from five years teaching in an elementary school in the nation's capitol. Living deeply—mentally, and physically—in this high-poverty world rattled me and caused me to challenge my assumptions regarding race and education. Any belief I had was held under the blazing light of poverty. Poverty, childhood trauma, hunger, PTSD, family instability, and economic stress weave through all levels of the school. These elements of poverty profoundly affect both a teacher's ability to effectively teach and a child's capacity to learn and grow.

The teachers are the key; they are the conduits. Teachers must be embraced as allies in the reform process. A system that haphazardly attacks teachers instead of nurturing their talents will constantly be in turmoil. Such a system can't make sustainable progress. It undermines and under-leverages its most valuable assets. Most teachers who made the commitment with me were dogged in their pursuit of helping our students succeed. I've painted these portraits of us in action to show the deep contradictions that lie within high-poverty schools. By working shoulder to shoulder with these teachers, I learned to be more vulnerable and resilient and to challenge my unconscious biases.

All children want to succeed, all children want to belong. Until we create a system that can help children experience the intrinsic value of education, one that excites wonder and curiosity, we will never realize our goals. To continue to plow ahead blindly, focused mainly on test scores, is a costly error. We must enact policies that embrace the whole child and then follow through on our commitments to children with fidelity. By taking a bottom-up approach that provides adequate social services as well as necessary instructional interventions, we can ensure that children who need the most support receive the help they need. By starting with these children, there will be fewer behavioral issues, and the rest of the school will be able to function more smoothly, being empowered to move beyond mere survival and create a true growth-oriented environment.

Epilogue

Music in the Halls is not a book that you can prepare yourself to read; maybe I was a little overly ambitious, thinking I could absorb it all in one sitting. From the introduction, the reader is drawn into the author's world, one of high pressure/high stakes, where immediate outcomes are demanded, yet distancing occurs between the adults and students within the school. *Music in the Halls* is a memoir, a documentary, and a wakeup call neatly packaged into one text.

There is something nostalgic and familiar, comforting even, about these stories of days in the life of a school, seen through one teacher's eyes. But there is also something that reeks of such sadness and emptiness that feels ongoing, never-ending, and overwhelming. As the reader, you quickly realize the parallel process happening. Author Bernard Jankowski opens the book writing about sharpening pencils and ends with how personal this experience was, as he himself is being sharpened. I reflected on that example of parallel process: fresh, new, untouched pencils and teachers being molded, formed, conformed, and made purposeful.

Poetry is interspersed among the narrative about students displaying oppositional, defiant behavior against the backdrop of compounded deprivations. We learn how much Jankowski, like many of his colleagues, works overtime, sacrificing their own breaks and self-care moments while simultaneously feeling like they can't do enough to meet the students' needs. The school described reads more like an emergency room environment. Students want to be self-determining, yet are absent, and when present, display outbursts, and lack emotional regulation, most of it learned trauma responses, all of it reflecting a desire still for connection.

I scribble responses on every page, reminders of *Lean on Me*, Spike Lee, and *Abbott Elementary* pictured in my mind.

What fear, terror, and intimidation in a life-or-death situation. One of intimacy, crying, violence, anger, animalistic desperation, and isolation. What do we really believe and are we living it out?

No one cares. The system is very much intent on self-preservation above all else. The only truth to be spoken is that of inequities and racism, Adverse Childhood Experience (ACE) scores at ten, and dedicated educators pushing to demonstrate and infuse strength, mission, and a sense of family into themselves, one another, and the students.

No one is considering how to strive, but just how to stay alive, not fully aware of how we only use the term *survive* when referring to a life-threatening illness, war, or other clearly traumatic happenings. There is a bouncing back and forth, an incessant game in which trust is elusive and immediate gratification rules the day. Unwanted exposure is pervasive.

Jankowski speaks of the early marginalization of boys, many diagnosed with learning or emotional/behavioral disabilities. How many more examples do we need of the school-to-prison pipeline? Juggling shame, embarrassment, guilt, and a desire to be different, worry was a constant, persistent, primary thief. The students and teachers alike internalized the stress, grief, and pain. Where is the wellness or work-life balance? Still, there was resilience that the overworked, underpaid teachers demonstrated in *Music in the Halls*. They could and would outlast. They built teams for mentorship, accountability, partnership, and camaraderie. They remained agile, flexible, and focused. Rather than adopt the competitive, unsustainable approach of their administration, these educators believed that "when teachers are selflessly committed to the children and the special education students are being adequately served, everyone benefits." They found their own language with the students, one of love and check in on you care. They leveraged humor despite inescapable tension. They knew what schools could be.

Notes and scribbles from the margins:

No one is left out. Every adult will make an impression on

the students and becomes a potential partner for their success.

Lack of technology

Awe of many proportions

Representation matters

Power of education, feeling seen

Luck is unpredictable and unreliable.

There is a recreation, vision, reclaiming.

What's valued in this community? What do we do with books? Does it seem useless? What do we choose to make space for? Not reading puts us in danger.

Quote from Rabbi: father would not trust his daughter marrying a boy who had no books in their house.

Life cycles depend on environmental norms and allowances.

Judgment? Looking for hope and authenticity?

How often does "the administration insists" on things that are irrelevant and unreasonable for the students and teachers?

Reclaiming lost boys

Community to the rescue

Named "The Rock" like a prison.

Revolutionary War, enemy language

The undermining of teamwork and overlooking of competence

There was an expiration date for "this untethered educational experiment." Such a flawed system.

Similar to Sisyphus

Written life poetry, the play on words and double entendre

Use of metaphors and analogy is brilliant and picturesque.

Paulo Freire, in the classic *Pedagogy of the Oppressed*, said, "Those who authentically commit themselves to the people must re-examine themselves constantly. This conversion is so radical as not to allow of ambiguous behavior." Jankowski is one of those who has authentically committed, having had many come-to-Jesus moments of humbling, choosing to confront himself, to increase his self-awareness, and to submit to continuous self-interrogation.

What does it mean to be a suburban white man in a school

building populated by Black and Brown children for whom poverty, instability, insecurity, and uncertainty is the norm? Culture, language, race, ethnicity, skin color, background, disability status, hungry or full, so many divides. So many questions. Yet, mindfulness calls us to be present. Jankowski doesn't miss the joy, the music, the creativity, the community, the self-expression, all that is and all who are bright and lovely. This embracing of what is moves us. Unpredictability reframed as spontaneity. Contrasts and tensions, the both-and of real life, complex and nuanced.

Richard Shaull, in the foreword to *Pedagogy of the Oppressed* by Paulo Freire, states:

"There is no such thing as a *neutral* educational process. Education either functions as an instrument that is used to facilitate the integration of the younger generation into the logic of the present system and bring about conformity to it, *or* it becomes 'the practice of freedom,' the means by which men and women deal critically and creatively with reality and discover how to participate in the transformation of their world."

Jankowski confronts us repeatedly, which education do we want? Which education do we value? "We expect a curiosity for learning to magically spring from this turbulent terrain filled with imminent, real, and embedded danger. We are the fools." Don't be the fool. It is unacceptable for ninety-eight of one hundred students to fail year after year. And now, after the COVID-19 pandemic, virtual learning, and every assortment of challenge known to human beings, this book, this call to action is more relevant than before. Do not simply put down this book after you have read the last word. Decide in this moment how you will live with a focus on "social emotional needs more than strict education."

Marja Humphrey, PhD, NCC, LGPC
Assistant Professor, School Counseling
Bowie State University